MILITARY DORSET
TODAY

By the same author:

Isle of Wight Railways: a 'then and now' photographic survey
Silver Link Publishing Ltd, 1991 (ISBN 0 947971 62 9)

British Railways Past and Present Special: Isle of Wight
Past & Present Publishing Ltd, 1993 (ISBN 1 85895 004 X)

The Bermuda Railway: Gone - But Not Forgotten!
Colin A. Pomeroy, 1993. (ISBN 0 9521298 0 9)

MILITARY DORSET TODAY

Second World War scenes and settings that can still be seen 50 years on

Colin A. Pomeroy

Published by the author
in association with

Silver Link Publishing Ltd

'In summary' - seen from an *Army* pillbox below Fort Upton is the Isle of Portland, its *Royal Navy* harbour and the skies in which the *Royal Air Force* fought the Battle of Britain in the summer of 1940 (OS: SY 831803).

© Colin A. Pomeroy 1995

ISBN 1 85794 077 6

Edited, designed and produced by the Book Packaging Department of
Silver Link Publishing Ltd
Unit 5
Home Farm Close
Church Street
Wadenhoe
Peterborough PE8 5TE
Tel/fax (01832) 720440

First published in September 1995

Printed and bound in Great Britain

British Library Cataloguing in Publication Data

A catalogue record for this book is available from the British Library.

CONTENTS

Note The following symbols after a listing indicate that the entry also contains information from another category (only some of which are shown in this Contents):

- **Ⓐ** Army and associated facilities
- **Ⓑ** Industry
- **Ⓒ** Memorials
- **Ⓓ** Museums
- **Ⓔ** Royal Air Force
- **Ⓕ** Royal Navy and associated facilities

FOREWORD

by
The Lord Digby, JP
Lord Lieutenant of the County of Dorset
and Honorary Colonel, 4th Battalion Devonshire & Dorset Regiment

I can well remember a family picnic at Came Down, between Weymouth and Dorchester, on our way to an Auxiliary Territorial Service (ATS) Parade on the morning of Sunday 3 September 1939. As we sat enjoying the late summer sunshine, we tuned in to hear Prime Minister Neville Chamberlain's sombre tones declare '. . .consequently this country is at war with Germany'.

This was a precursor to nearly six years of frantic activity in the beautiful County of Dorset, which would only end with the defeat of Germany, Japan and their allies and the freedom from tyranny that we enjoy today; as this book shows, Dorset was to play an extremely important part in this ultimately successful campaign. My own family home was taken over at a week's notice to house the Royal Naval Hospital, which had been bombed in Portland. My father and I both served in the Coldstream Guards, my mother and sister in the ATS and, whilst waiting to be called up, I served in the Home Guard - then called the Local Defence Volunteers.

Despite its peaceful pastoral image, Dorset has always played a major part in our country's military activities. Local ships sailing forth to meet the Spanish Armada, the Dorset Regiment fighting below our National Colours across the globe, and Dorset's efforts - both offensive and supportive - during the Great War are all examples of such activity prior to the Second World War.

As time slips by and other events occupy our minds, I am most pleased that Colin Pomeroy has given us this book as a timely reminder of our County's part in the great national effort of 1939 to 1945, and, most importantly, drawn attention to many of the artifacts remaining to be seen today. It was essential that someone recorded this information, before those who can draw upon memories of the installations covered pass on to a greater life.

Our County Badge features a castle, and its motto 'Who's Afear'd' indicates a spirit of bravery. I trust that you will find in this book full evidence of the strength and bravery shown in Dorset in our nation's time of greatest need.

Minterne, Dorset

ACKNOWLEDGEMENTS

So many people have helped me in the collecting of data for this book that it would take a chapter in itself to list them all and state in which way each so kindly offered assistance!

In alphabetical order, may I place on record my thanks to the following, whilst offering my sincere apologies to anyone who has contacted me but I have not listed:

Mr C. Ashworth, Mr T. Austin, Lieutenant Commander M. Batty, Mr A. Bailey, Ms J. Bembridge, Squadron Leader R. Breward, Mr J. Bush, Mr G. Chard, Squadron Leader P. Christopher MBE DFC, Commonwealth War Graves Commission, Mr B. Cox, Mr & Mrs N. Dicks, Lord Edward Digby, Directorate of Public Relations (Navy), Dorchester Public Library, Dorset County Council, Dorset County Records Office, Mr P. Duff, Major N. Dunkley MBE, Group Captain Sir Edward Fennessy CBE, Mr J. Geddes, Mr A. Glanville, Mr & Mrs B. Guest, Squadron Leader C. Halstead, Mr D. Hawthornthwaite, Mr J. Hoskins, Mr B. Hunter-Inglis, The Imperial War Museum, Mr & Mrs J. Isaac, Mr W. Jones, Lychett Minster School, Mr A. McDonald, Mrs E. McElwaine, Maiden Newton Community Trust, Mr H. Marshall, Mr J. Masters, Mr N. Meech, Mr H. Merriman, Lieutenant Commander S. O'Reilly, Major M. Parmley, Major R. Pickard, Mr G. Pickford, Mrs M. Pinset, Public Records Office, Kew, Mr I. Robertson, Wing Commander D. Ryan, Mr F. Simpson, Mr D. Snowdon, Wing Commander K. Soal, Mr I. Strange, Mr R. Stubbington, Mrs J. Taylor, Mrs P. Tharby, Mrs F. Treasure, Captain C. Walker, Mrs E. Walker, Mrs M. Ward, Weymouth Public Library, and Colonel J. Woodward.

Finally, I must thank my dear wife 'Binks', who, as always, has shown patience and understanding as I've wandered off to do my own thing (or sat for hours at the keyboard).

INTRODUCTION

Travelling around beautiful Dorset, it is impossible not to come across reminders of the county's military history from years long gone: impressive Maiden Castle, rugged Corfe Castle and the walls surrounding the town of Wareham are but three examples of this - and all these, and very much more, are already well recorded for present and future generations to read about and give thought to. The county's history during the Second World War has also been well chronicled, but what has been missing is information on what remains to be seen in Dorset today from that conflict. This I have tried to go some way towards rectifying, and specifically while those who can remember those awesome days in the years from 1939 to 1945 are still with us to pass on their memories.

What follows in the pages to come is not a definitive listing of what can still be seen from the days of the Second World War, for there is too much still to be encountered, in varying states of good repair or poor decay, to list in a book such as this. One could, I suspect, write a book on Dorset pillboxes and Dragon's Teeth alone! What I have tried to do is give the reader a flavour of the artifacts that remain - no more - but of sufficient diversity to be both meaningful and, I trust, interesting.

All three of the armed services had strong connections with the county. Today only the Army remains in Dorset in any strength and with any long-term future, for the Royal Navy is preparing to abandon the base at Portland in 1996, and the associated helicopter airfield in 1999, and the RAF's presence has, operationally, gone altogether. Thus the demise of two of our three fighting forces within the county is another reason to put pen to paper now, for unless there is a major change in Government policy towards the armed services or - shudder the thought - we slip back into a Cold War situation, folk will soon forget just how important the county once was in military terms. Equally, the 'Peace Dividend' has seen a decline in Dorset's industrial and research & development importance to the defence industry.

On turning the pages to follow, it will soon become evident that there is very much more listed in connection with the southern coastal belt of Dorset than there is for the rest of the county. This is not an attempt, as someone born and bred in Weymouth, to be parochial, but the simple fact is that it was in this area of Dorset that most of the military activity took place. In the dark, early days of the war it was here that the pitifully small response that the country could offer to any German invader was mustered to do its desperate best; as the county moved from a bastion of defence to become a springboard for attack, it was again on the coast - near to the ports - that the complex structures necessary to move the Allied armies across the Channel were drawn up and the forces themselves concentrated.

Equally, the RAF's ground-based navigation transmitters were placed as far south as possible to give maximum reception range to aircraft operating over continental Europe, and its radars were similarly positioned to give the maximum warning of approaching aircraft. Nevertheless, there were precious few places within Dorset that were completely untouched by the armed conflict - as the many memorials in the county to those who gave their lives in the cause of King and Country most poignantly illustrate.

In drawing on written and spoken memories of over half a century ago, there will inevitably be errors of fact or emphasis in the book. Where conflicting evidence has been uncovered, I have used my judgement to try and resolve the differences - supported, when possible, by recollections of those present at the time (although, even here, people's memories have given me different versions of the same events!) So, finally, I accept full responsibility for any errors that remain and offer my apologies accordingly.

Since the end of the war Dorset's boundaries have changed, with Bournemouth, Christchurch and other areas of the east of the county having been transferred from Hampshire to Dorset in the 1974 Local Government Boundary Review. At the time of writing change is also in the air, with both Bournemouth and Poole to become unitary authorities in their own right. Within these pages I have considered for entry places that were in 'current' Dorset in 1995.

In using this book, if you wish to visit the listed locations to see for yourself these mementos of yesteryear, it will be useful to have access to good maps, and the following 1:50,000 Ordnance Survey sheets are recommended:

183 (Yeovil & Frome)
184 (Salisbury & The Plain)
193 (Taunton & Lyme Regis)
194 (Dorchester and Weymouth)
195 (Bournemouth & Purbeck)

The vast majority of sites I have listed are readily visible from the highway, public footpaths or similar places, and only in a few locations is the ability to view (as opposed to gain access) restricted. I would respectfully ask readers to please avoid infringing on any privacies and, equally, to avoid trespassing at all costs. Thank you.

Please, as you read through the pages that follow, remember the sacrifices made by Dorset men and women, and by the innumerable Allied combatants who served in our county (from both within and without our island shores) in gaining for us the freedoms we enjoy today. It is with these brave patriots in mind that I leave you to enjoy this book.

Colin Pomeroy
Clyffe, Dorchester
August 1995

Portland Postcript

The run-down of the naval base is now almost complete. On Friday 21 July 1995, to a 13-gun salute, led by the Naval Tug *Adept* (A224) and escorted by 10 other auxiliary vessels and the Weymouth Lifeboat, HMS *Argyll* - F231, a Duke Class frigate - sailed through the East Ship Channel with Flag Officer Sea Training embarked en route for his staff's new base at Devonport, bringing the Royal Navy's 150-year seaborne association with Portland to a virtual close. Although the helicopter base is scheduled to stay in operation until 1999, the vast majority of the dockyard and harbour has been sold to the company Portland Port, which is seeking to redevelop the area by providing bulk cargo and roll-on roll-off ferry facilities, associated marine services, a fuel oil handling terminal, cruise ship berthing and the like.

ROYAL NAVY
AND OTHER
MARITIME FACILITIES

GODLINGSTON HILL

OS: SZ 005807

Location: At and on Godlingston Hill, above Knitson Farm, which is located on the minor road running parallel to the A351 and B3351 roads running from Corfe Castle to Swanage and Studland.

Work on this major site began in 1936 (which resulted in Knitson Farm itself being the first in the valley to receive a mains electricity supply!). Although I have included this facility in the naval section of the book, it had many Army and RAF associations as well - for example the RAF's J Watch personnel, who monitored German communications.

Godlingston Hill was a major communications unit, with an emphasis on shipping (and, to a lesser extent, aircraft) in distress, and also had an important role in providing 'behind the front' battlefield communications, much of a highly sensitive nature. It was designated as a communications facility for forces involved in Operation 'Overlord', and saw considerable activity in this role - with US Navy personnel joining those of the Navy, Army and RAF already based there. During those early days of the action on mainland Europe - when it was felt by those in authority that the enemy might try to land saboteurs on the Dorset coast to disrupt these vital communications - the complex was guarded each night by skilled personnel of the local Auxiliary Unit. Then, as the war in Europe moved inland from the

Still in use today - the easternmost hilltop site. Note the old transmitter base in the right foreground.

French coast, the unit's importance diminished and by 1945 it is reputed to have been reduced to a care and maintenance status.

Today this previously secret military site has many interesting artifacts for the enthusiast to view. In the garden of Old Knitson farmhouse there still stand two of the three Nissen huts once located there as domestic accommodation, as well as a former latrine block now in use as a garden shed. There are also four of the operational buildings remaining, all set in to the hill above the farm.

To reach them, take the public footpath alongside the old farmhouse (signposted 'Nine Barrow Down') and continue past the gate until the path splits; take the right-hand path and continue until you reach the lower of the remaining buildings, which is readily accessible. Next, continue in the same direction, until the path splits again - at which point keep left and climb to the top of the hill. You will now be able to see the other three structures; two are abandoned but the third is still in communications use as an aerial site for both local radio and government communications.

The lower bunker, which was manned by Army personnel and contained the unit telephone exchange. The track leading to the higher level bunkers is clearly visible beyond.

Inside the lower bunker - effectively a buried Nissen hut.

ROYAL NAVAL AIR STATION, HENSTRIDGE

OS: ST 522025

Location: Off the A30 trunk road from Sherborne to Shaftesbury, some 2 miles east of the traffic lights in the village of Henstridge.

Work commenced on the building of a five-runway airfield on this farmland site in the summer of 1941, the airfield being specifically laid out for the training of pilots destined to fly on carrier-born operations. The building process was somewhat long-winded, and it was not until April 1943 that RNAS Henstridge, commissioned as HMS *Dipper*, became fully operational.

For all of its wartime years Henstridge was involved in flying training, operating a variety of aircraft, the most noteworthy being Seafires, the naval version of the Spitfire. One interesting peculiarity at Henstridge was the short runway laid out as an aircraft carrier flight deck, complete with arrester wires. Thus Henstridge could boast parallel runways well before London/Heathrow!

Like so many wartime airfields, Henstridge was run down when hostilities ceased, but in 1949 it was taken over by nearby RNAS Yeovilton (HMS *Heron*) as a satellite airfield, and continued thus until 1952, and again from 1954 to 1957, when it finally closed to military flying.

There is nowhere more melancholy than an abandoned airfield - but happily, although but a shadow of its former self, Henstridge still sees a limited amount of flying from its aged runways and is not nearly so sad a place as many of its contemporaries! In the order of 25 private aircraft can be found at there today, so the skies still reverberate to the sound of throaty piston engines. From a military history point of view, the most fascinating

Henstridge Tower today, still showing very obvious signs of its original design purpose.

must be the beautifully restored Westland Lysander V92981, which is based here.

There is also much else to see - numerous hangars, the control tower (now a private house), revetments, air raid shelters, fuel installations, gun butts and the like - much more in the way of military artifacts from yesteryear than would be the case if the whole airfield had been returned to farming or completely covered with industrial units. Even the majority of the dummy deck landing installation is still in situ!

Note: Much of Henstridge airfield lies within the County of Somerset; nevertheless, enough lies within Dorset for this fascinating airfield to be included within these pages.

Of not dissimilar vintage to the gun harmonising butts in the background, Luscombe 'Special' G-AKTI taxies in towards the Second World War hangars after flight.

A bulk fuel installation point on the western side of the airfield. Bowsers would refill here before proceeding to the aircraft waiting for fuel.

Henstridge light aircraft line-up, with an equally impressive line-up of wartime buildings in the background.

MOTOR CRUISER *MY GIRL*

> Location: *My Girl* sails out of Weymouth Harbour from a site near the Timewalk Museum. Out of season she can usually be seen tied up in Weymouth's Inner Harbour.

My Girl was built in 1937 as a pleasure cruiser for holidaymakers in the resort town of Weymouth and was licensed to carry 66 passengers on trips around Weymouth Bay and Portland Harbour. As a lad, I can well remember *My Girl* working with other vessels of the White Motor Boats partnership from the pontoon of ex-military barges alongside the (now partly demolished) Pier Bandstand.

During the war, under the control of the naval authorities but under the command of her skipper Ron Hill, *My Girl* was employed in ferrying men and materials out to the forts and installations on the breakwater arms of Portland Harbour - in all weathers, by night and by day, and on occasions when the air was filled with shrapnel and splinters! Her wartime log records over 20,000 sea miles in military service, and the carriage of over 250,000 troops - plus large amounts of freight. In 1944, in appreciation of her support of the breakwater gun positions, she was presented with a Royal Artillery pennant. Her adventures are chronicled in the book *Weymouth at War - Ron Hill's story of the vessel 'My Girl'* (see the Bibliography).

Today, still fitted with the cabin that was built on to her in the war years and back with a gleaming white hull and light varnish upperworks instead of wartime grey, the pristine *My Girl* continues to carry Weymouth visitors to sea and out to her old wartime haunts in and around Portland Harbour. Now owned by Skipper Ian Robertson, *My Girl* is a proud vessel with a distinguished wartime record.

With the quayside buildings of Weymouth Harbour behind her, *My Girl* prepares to come alongside her mooring for another day's pleasure cruising.

POOLE HARBOUR   OS: SZ 006903 (Poole Bridge)

Location: Between the town of Poole and the Isle of Purbeck.

For all of the war years Poole Harbour - its quays, waterways, shoreline, and the airspace overhead - was a scene of frantic activity. (See also separate entries for RNAS Sandbanks (page 25), Poole boat yards (page 120), Brownsea Island (page 39), Brownsea Island Decoy Site (page 95), RAF Hamworthy (page 101), RN Cordite Factory (page 121) and St James's church, Poole (page 142).) During the period of the 'Phoney War' the facilities on and around the harbour were readied for the fighting that was still to come, with defensive measures tied in with those being taken to defend the whole of the Poole peninsula and utilising both the Home Guard and locally based troops and naval personnel. When the evacuation of the British Expeditionary Force from Dunkirk became inevitable, small ships from Poole, including the RNLI lifeboat *Thomas Kirk Wright*, set off to join the hastily assembled armada of

rescue vessels that brought some 338,000 troops off the beaches and harbour walls.

As the war progressed the various RN, Army and RAF units at Poole underwent many changes, but by the end of 1943 Poole Harbour and its facilities were fully committed to the work involved in readying our armed forces, and those of our locally based allies, for the return to Europe. The RN Port Control Authority waged a continual battle for more and more space to contain the vast number of assault craft that were being assembled here - many having been built locally - for training exercises and, ultimately, Operation 'Overlord'. The Combined Operations Base, HMS *Turtle*, took over the site at Lake previously occupied by RAF Hamworthy, with the Combined Operations mentor Lord Louis Mountbatten being amongst the regular senior visitors to Poole to view progress.

Trials for PLUTO (Pipe Line Under The Ocean), which was to feed fuel oils to our forces in France from a final UK pumping stations at Shanklin and Sandown on the Isle of Wight, were conducted in Poole Bay; other local trials

The commemorative plaque on the wall of the old Customs House, on The Quay.

involved the using of landing craft as rocket, anti-aircraft and gun platforms, making use of these crafts' shallow drafts to enable them to get close inshore to enemy-held beaches. In May of 1944 some 60 rescue cutters of the US Coastguard arrived at Poole to provide a rescue and casualty evacuation service.

Then D-Day arrived and Poole Harbour saw its complex sea traffic plans work well as the local element of the invasion fleet, with minesweepers leading the way, left for the assembly area south of St Catherine's Point. For the rest of the war Poole harbour and its numerous facilities supported the Allies' push towards the German homeland and victory, in Europe, on 8 May 1945.

Well before final victory had been achieved, with the surrender of Japan on 12 September, the vast majority of the military presence at Poole had gone and the process of removing Nissen huts, other temporary buildings, and disposing of surplus vessels was well under way. Poole Harbour had the honour of welcoming home the first of the ex-POWs from the inhumane Japanese camps, when they arrived on 18 September by flying boat then left for London by rail.

RAF Air Sea Rescue Unit

A Royal Air Force Air Sea Rescue Marine Craft Unit was also based in the harbour, at Salternes Pier (OS: SZ 036897) for the final two years of the war. No 36 ASR MCU was not officially opened until 17 April 1944, but had already been in action on 25 March, when 24 personnel were saved from a locally ditched glider.

A particularly brave rescue was that carried out on 2 June 1944, when the crew of a ditched Walrus aircraft was rescued just 10 miles off Cherbourg. In addition to the 'alert craft' alongside at Poole, ASR high-speed launches (HSLs) were, weather permitting, regularly stationed off Durlston Head to reduce transit times to downed aircraft.

Today Poole Harbour is still a scene of hectic activity, but of a much more peaceful kind. The only military presence on its shores is the Royal Marines base at Hamworthy, still using a limited number of the wartime facilities. The vessels that ply the seaways once thronged by landing craft and other ships of war are commercial ferries and coasters working, mainly, cross-Channel routes, together with vast numbers of pleasure craft.

The remains of two Mk 4 Tank Landing Craft, each capable of carrying nine tanks, beached alongside the oil jetty since the mid-1950s. One carries the pennant number LcT (4) 510.

PORTLAND
ROYAL NAVY BASE
OS: SY 688745 (Main Gate)

Location: The southern shore of
Portland Harbour.

Although men o' war and their attendant vessels have taken refuge in the sheltered waters between Weymouth and the Isle of Portland since man first went to sea to wage war, it was only in 1845 that Queen Victoria's Government appointed a Royal Commission to consider providing artificial protection for these and other vessels.

Following completion of the refuge, warships of the Royal Navy and our allies operated from Portland in active participation in, or support of, all British military operations that were to follow. During the Great War the base saw service as an anchorage for capital vessels as well as the lair from which RN destroyers and other small, fast craft could venture out in to the English Channel in search of their prey. From 1917 seaplanes were based within the harbour to fly anti-submarine patrols - a foretaste of today's naval air station.

Never, however, was the Royal Navy base at Portland more important than during the Second World War, when it made a major contribution to the Allied effort, initially in a defensive posture as Britain absorbed punishment as a result of the Nazi successes in mainland Europe, later in a much more offensive way as the war swung in the Allies' favour, and finally, from 6 June 1944 to the end of European hostilities, in support of Operation 'Overlord', during which 418,585 troops and 144,093 vehicles passed through Portland *en route* to French and, later, Belgian ports and beachheads.

Today this previously important base is in the process of being run down as part of the shrinking of our armed forces in the aftermath of the ending of the Cold War; the dockyard and main base is due to be given up in 1996 and the airfield in 1999. Very many wartime installations remain, and will continue to do so for many years to come. The wartime additions on the breakwaters contrast quite markedly with

The hard at which large numbers of assault and support craft were loaded before setting sail for the beaches of Normandy from 6 June 1944 until the European War's end. One of Dorset's most ugly buildings - the 'new' wardroom - dominates the skyline behind the more typical Portland houses on the road leading towards the main dockyard gate.

Two sections of Phoenix Caissons (Mulberry Harbour breakwaters) afloat off Casteltown Pier.

the original defensive positions built there, while of course many of the pre-1939 structures saw war service in the period covered by this book. The main hard used for loading invasion craft was a wartime addition to the base facilities, and is now used as a repair slipway, while two Phoenix Caissons from the successful Mulberry Harbour project remain off the jetty built in 1950 - having been positioned there as some protection during its construction

The base hospital is now used by the Dorset National Health Trust, and the impressive former Grand Canteen is used for administrative and operational purposes, with - most unusually - the airfield air traffic control tower being located on its roof. The airfield was not there during the war - this area was a mere - and where the main gate to HMS *Osprey* now stands was Portland railway station (as the plaque there shows).

The earliest of the oil tanks on the causeway across to Weymouth date from 1901; during the war they were encased in protective concrete, but to ease maintenance this was stripped off in later years. A successful daytime decoy site at Chickerell, a replica of the Portland tanks, drew German raiders away from here and the real fuel tanks were never damaged by bombing. A night decoy site was also established to the north of Weymouth on open ground at Littlemoor.

The breakwater defences

Construction of the three vast breakwater arms that enclose the harbour of Portland was commenced in 1849, when Prince Albert laid the first stone of what is now called the Inner Arm (the southernmost of the trio). This was completed in 1872 and shortly afterwards it was agreed to enclose fully the anchorage with two additional arms, and these were completed by 1902 and 1904. The massive structures protected the fleet against the worst of the elements, but could not do so against a resolute enemy - particularly one equipped with torpedo-firing surface and sub-surface vessels.

The major defensive position to be built to achieve the required security was the Breakwater Fort (the Chequer or Chequered Fort), a 116-foot-diameter circular iron structure with adjacent barracks; other protection was afforded by land-based forts. Additionally, in 1914 the veteran battleship HMS *Hood* was sunk to block off the southern harbour entrance to German submarines or motor torpedo boats. Quick-firing guns were located at the other two seaways, together with powerful searchlights, to deter enemy vessels from forcing these passages, and dolphins (booms) were also provided. Additionally the north and middle arms were equipped with a range of, then, state-of-the-art weaponry.

Prior to and during the Second World War the fortifications on the breakwaters were updated to carry later armaments; the Breakwater Fort, for example, was equipped with two 6-inch guns, and the gun positions at 'A' and 'C' pierheads each had a pair of 12-pounder guns (an ideal gun for use against fast craft). The fort at the end of the inner arm had seen little use over the years, particularly since the *Hood* was sunk below its granite walls, but was equipped with a 40 mm Bofors gun during this period.

Good views of the dockyard can be obtained from many directions, the best two being from one of the pleasure boats that ply for trade from Weymouth or from the top of the island, either by the Portland Heights Hotel or the north gate of the Verne Prison. The Mulberry Harbour caissons are best seen from the public road leading to Dockyard Gate. In the fullness of time, when the site becomes civilianised, it is most likely that more of this historic naval base and dockyard will be open to the public.

Right **Breakwater Lighthouse, viewed from seaward, with 20th-century additions to the breakwater defences very obvious.**

Below **The Inner Arm Fort, looking seaward across Weymouth Bay to the Purbeck coastline.**

Below right **Portland has many underground installations, many of them still not revealed to the public gaze. This is one of two entrances to an operations block and attack shelter off the main internal dockyard road.**

ROYAL NAVY SHIPS BEARING DORSET NAMES

During the Second World War various vessels bore names associated with the County of Dorset:

HMS *Dorsetshire*, the third Royal Navy vessel to carry the county name, was a 'Norfolk' Class cruiser. She obtained fame when delivering the *coup de grâce* to the *Bismarck* on 27 May 1941, but was sunk during a Japanese air attack on Colombo Harbour on 5 April 1942.

HMS *Cattistock* was a 'Hunt' Class destroyer. She was launched in February 1940 and scrapped in 1957.

HMS *Blackmore* was a Type II 'Hunt' Class destroyer. She was launched in December 1941 and sold to the Royal Norwegian Navy in 1952, where she was renamed *Esbern Snare*; she was scrapped in 1966.

HMS *Bridport* was a 'Bangor' Class minesweeping sloop, launched in February 1940, transferred to the RAF as a tender to the Joint Anti-Submarine School in 1946 and broken up in 1958.

HMS *Cape Portland* (a 'Cape' Class fishing vessel, hence the unusual terminology for Portland Bill) was requisitioned from her owners in 1939 and converted for anti-submarine duties. She also saw service as an armed boarding vessel and, after a couple of years with the Portuguese Navy, returned to fishing in 1945.

HMS *Lulworth* was an American Coastguard cutter (ex-USCG *Chelan*). She saw wartime service with the Royal Navy and was returned to her original owners in January 1946.

HMS *Lyme Regis* was another vessel of the 'Bangor' Class, launched in February 1941, transferred to the Royal Indian Navy the next year and scrapped in her 20th year afloat.

A second HMS *Lyme Regis*, as a result of the renaming of HMS *Sunderland*, was launched in March 1942 and, ironically, broken up in Sunderland in 1948. The ship's bell and ensign of the second vessel are now laid up in the Church of St Michael the Archangel in the town of Lyme Regis.

HMS *Poole* was also a 'Bangor' Class vessel; she was launched in June 1941 and scrapped in January 1948.

HMS *Maiden Castle*, a 'Castle' Class corvette, was launched in June 1944, but was not commissioned in this name, seeing service as the *Empire Lifeguard* - initially as a convoy rescue ship and, after the war, as a troopship.

HMS *Sherborne Castle*, of the same Class, was transferred to the Royal Canadian Navy shortly after having been launched in February 1944 and saw service with the Canadians as HMCS *Tunsberg*.

HMS *Frome* was a 'River' Class frigate; she was launched in June 1943, then transferred to the French Navy as *L'Escarmouche*.

HMS *Portland Bill* was a Depot & Repair ship, launched in May 1945 and transferred to the merchant navy in 1951, where she bore the name *Zinnia*.

HMS *Stour* was a 'Mersey' Class armed trawler, launched in 1917 and sold off in 1945.

Although not a Royal Navy vessel, the **MV *Dorset*** also deserves a mention; she was one of only five ships to survive the 'Ohio Convoy', which brought desperately needed salvation to the island fortress of Malta in August 1942.

Today two ships of the Royal Navy still proudly carry Dorset names: HMS *Bridport* and HMS *Cattistock*.

HMS *Bridport*

The present HMS *Bridport* - pennant number M105 - is the fifth of the 'Sandown' Class of minehunters. She was built at the Thorneycroft Yard in Southampton, launched on 30 July 1992 and first commissioned into the Royal Navy at the Portland Naval Base on 6 November 1993.

HMS *Bridport* is built of extremely strong glass reinforced plastic (GRP), highly manoeuvrable and dedicated to the minehunting and disposal role. She has a displacement of 485 tonnes and, in addition to her mine disposal apparatus, is armed with a quick-firing 30 mm gun and light machine guns.

HMS *Cattistock*

Commissioned in 1982, the present HMS *Cattistock* - pennant number M31 - is a 'Hunt' Class mine countermeasures ves-

HMS *Bridport* at Dartmouth, with the Britannia Royal Naval College in the background.

HMS *Cattistock* in a moderate sea off the Dorset coastline.

sel, capable of both sweeping for mines and hunting for them with the ship's sonar. With a displacement of 625 tons she is, like HMS *Bridport*, built of GRP and carries a similar armament fit.

Finally, although not bearing a Dorset name, HMS *Pine* is worthy of mention here.

Launched in March 1940, this 530-ton 'Tree' Class Mine Sweeping Trawler was adopted by the town of Gillingham in January 1942, which had held a fund-raising 'Warship Week' the previous November and raised over £110,000. Her main defensive armament was a 12 lb gun, mounted in the bows, so she was completely outgunned by the German E-boat that sunk her in the English Channel in October 1943 (but with many of the crew surviving).

Today, in memory of the ship and her association with the town, a photograph of HMS *Pine* and a plaque hang on the wall in Gillingham Town Hall.

ROYAL NAVAL AIR STATION SANDBANKS

OS: SZ 044877

Location: Old Coastguard Road, off the circulatory road system on the approach to the Sandbanks Ferry.

The Royal Navy's air station at Sandbanks, on the spit of land forming the northern arm of the entrance to Poole Harbour, was commissioned as a satellite to HMS *Daedalus*, Lee-on-Solent, in May 1940, becoming fully operational in August of the same year. The base used the requisitioned premises of the Royal Motor Yacht Club, which had been in residence there since 1935. The Club House was used as the unit Headquarters and the boat shed alongside as a hangar, capable of taking 14 small seaplanes of the Walrus type. The only other facilities were a small repair shop and a concrete ramp and slipway leading down to the sheltered waters of Poole Harbour. Unofficially known as HMS *Tadpole* ('small frog' compared with the BOAC flying boat base!), this became the official name of the base in 1943.

The unit's primary task was as the Basic Seaplane Training School. No 765 Squadron of the Fleet Air Arm relocated here from Calshot when its base there was heavily bombed, bringing its remaining Walrus aircraft with it, while other types to operate from Sandbanks included Vought

In early wartime this building was in use as a seaplane hangar; now, as it was from 1935 to 1939, it is the RMYC boat shed.

Kingfishers and Fairey Seafoxes. Although primarily involved in the training of aircrew, the base occasionally dispatched aircraft on operational sorties, some of which were of a covert and clandestine nature. If weather conditions or operational necessity warranted it, aircraft were sometimes launched on the seaward side of the peninsula (adjacent to where the Sandbanks Beach car park now stands).

With the increase of flying boat activity in Poole Harbour, both military and civilian, as the war progressed the decision was made to close down RNAS Sandbanks, and the last unit here, 765 Squadron, disbanded on 15 October 1943. From then onwards the site was used as a landing craft base, with its main emphasis on pre-invasion training for the assault landings on the coast of Normandy that lay ahead. A force of motor gun boats (MGBs) was also based here for a time in 1944.

Today the facilities once again form the premises of the Royal Motor Yacht Club. The Club House is back in use as the headquarters of this prestigious club, which has HRH Prince Philip as its Admiral, and the once military hangar - with the notice still displayed on its wall as a warning to pilots and engineers alike, 'A HOT ENGINE IS ALWAYS ON CONTACT' - is again fulfilling its design purpose as a boat shed (but has recently been shortened and had the door relocated from the seaward end of the shed to the northern side).

The RMYC is only open to members and their guests; however, good views of the buildings can be seen both from the local public highways and from the waters of Poole Harbour.

The Club House today, having seen wartime service as the headquarters building for a naval air station and then a landing craft training unit.

WEYMOUTH HARBOUR OS: SY 685788

Location: A central position in the resort of Weymouth (well signposted).

The ancient port of Weymouth and Melcombe Regis has played a prominent part in our maritime history, including the sending of ships to join Sir Francis Drake's fleet in combat with the Spanish Armada in 1588. However, its military importance was never greater than during the Second World War. As the country braced itself for full combat during the days of the 'Phoney War', one of Dorset's first indications of things to come was the arrival at the port of over 23,000 refugees from the evacuated Channel Islands.

The Royal Navy shore base at Weymouth was commissioned as HMS *Bee*, and expanded rapidly. Contraband control vessels operated out of Weymouth (including the paddle steamers that plied their trade here in more peaceful times), escorting neutral vessels into the sheltered waters of the bay - and under the guns of the Nothe Fort - for cargo examinations. HMS *Bee* also acted as host to Coastal Forces vessels, namely the motor torpedo and motor gun boats that set sail nightly to seek contact with the enemy in waters across the Channel. It also acted as a working-up base for these fast and heavily armed craft.

In the autumn of 1943, as more and more space on the South Coast became

The harbour wall, with the Pavilion Theatre just visible on the right. It was down the steps seen clearly in this view that many of the United States Army personnel walked before embarking in the assault craft for the invasion of Normandy in June 1944.

needed for D-Day preparations, the majority of HMS *Bee*'s facilities were moved away, and the United States Navy took over the running of the base, initially as HMS *Grasshopper*, but from May 1944 as the Combined Operations base USS *Grasshopper*. Weymouth Harbour was then deeply involved in the training, and subsequent loading and dispatch, of assault craft destined for the Omaha landing beach in Normandy - and continued to support operations in Europe long after the last shots had been fired.

RAF Air Sea Rescue Unit

In addition to the naval vessels operating out of Weymouth, a Royal Air Force Air Sea Rescue Marine Craft Unit was also based here during the last two years of the war. No 40 ASR MCU opened at Weymouth on 6 April 1944 and continued to operate until disbandment on 2 August 1945, at which time it was equipped with three 67-foot high-speed launches (HSLs). The unit's headquarters and operations room were in the Customs House building,

personnel were accommodated at nearby RAF Chickerell and - when the necessity arose - the HSLs were hauled out of the water for repair or maintenance on the Great Western Railway slipway adjacent to the lifeboat station. The unit merited its establishment on one day alone, for on the morning of D-Day one of its launches saved the lives of 24 US troops whose glider had ditched off Portland Bill.

Today there is little left to show how busy, militarily, Weymouth harbour was some 50 years ago. The requisitioned harbourside buildings have long since been returned to their rightful owners and the multitude of temporary structures have long been removed. Nevertheless, viewed from alongside the harbour or from the ramparts of the Nothe Fort above, it is easy to imagine the intense activity here as contraband control vessels set out to investigate shipping in the Channel, MTBs left on raids in the Cherbourg area, or assault craft slipped out on the night of 5 June 1944, their next stop being the beaches of Normandy.

A general view of the harbour, with visiting Scottish trawlers and HM Customs Vessel *Sentinel* tied up where warships once lay alongside, and yachts standing where military vessels were once hauled out for battle damage repair. Note the Weymouth lifeboat; her wartime predecessor *The William and Clara Ryland* could only put to sea, even on life-saving missions, with permission from the Naval Port Control authorities.

ARMY
AND
ASSOCIATED FACILITIES

ANDERSON MANOR

OS: SY 880976

Location: On the outskirts of Winterborne Kingston, approached on an unclassified road from the A31 at 'Red Post'.

Ideally located near to Poole Harbour and to military training areas, yet well off the beaten track, Anderson Manor (built in 1622) was requisitioned early in the war as the Headquarters of the Special Operations Executive's Small Scale Raiding Force - established on Prime Minister Winston Churchill's specific instructions as a nuisance force to carry our raids on German-occupied territory. The SSRF carried out a series of highly successful raids, of which two are by far the best known: that on the Casquets Lighthouse in the Channel Islands on the night of 2/3 September 1942 when, in addition to capturing the German personnel manning the position, all the code books and military documents to hand were recovered safely to England; and the canoe raid on the shipping in the River Gironde at Bordeaux on 12 December of the same year - the story behind the film *Cockleshell Heroes*. As a further Dorset connection, it is worthy of mention that one of the four vessels sunk by the canoeists was the 7,132-ton SS *Portland*!

The SSRF disbanded in 1943, but Anderson Manor remained in SOE hands, known as Station 62, until hostilities were over. For the tough commando training that was carried out here, an out-

The house viewed from the beautiful formal gardens.

door firing range was located behind the house to the north, an indoor firing range - the base of which can still be seen today - in the western courtyard, and a strenuous obstacle course in the main driveway in front of the house.

Since the war years a few of those who served here in 'The Secret War' have returned to relive their memories, and the wall of the adjacent little church bears a brass plaque carrying the inscription: 'In Memory of the Small Scale Raiding Force (62 Commando) and all who served with the Special Operations Executive at Anderson Manor during the Second World War'.

Today the house is back in private ownership and not open to the public. However, glimpses - some fuller than others - can be had from the adjacent public footpath, nearby roads and the little churchyard. Additionally, note from the bridleway leading up to Muston Down the base of the shooting range mentioned above.

The interior of the tiny church. The nearer plaque is in memory of the SSRF personnel and the one on its right remembers Captain J. P. Young, of the King's Own Hussars, who was killed on active service in Cyprus on 17 September 1941.

AUXILIARY UNIT HIDES

Great Britain was the only country to have had a resistance movement established prior to an invasion or occupation, the organisation going under the intentionally ambiguous name of 'Auxiliary Units', with its communications branch being equally meaninglessly titled 'Special Duties Sections'. The highly secret Auxiliary Units were being established before war broke out, from local folk who had an intimate knowledge of their local countryside, and remained operational until the threat of Nazi invasion was over and a stand-down order was promulgated in November 1944.

By 1941 their were nearly 50 patrols, with 32 Operational Bases (built mainly by Pioneers of the Royal Engineers) established within Dorset, with over 300 members enlisted. These hideouts were 'go-to-ground' sites where the units would have hidden until the invading forces had passed them by, before emerging to create havoc in the enemy's lines of communication and supply & logistics organisation.

Initially the Headquarters of the Dorset Auxiliary Unit organisation, which was divided geographically into six areas, was at Bingham's Melcombe House, near the village of Melcombe Bingham; later in the war it was relocated to Duntish Court, near Buckland Newton. The standard OB consisted of one large room, which was 14 feet long, a small store room, cooking area and toilet and a passage leading off to an escape exit addi-

Auxiliary Unit Sergeant Fred Simpson stands in the main chamber of the remains of his patrol's Creech Barrow hide. Note, over his left shoulder, one of the ventilation pipes.

tional to the main entrance, which itself was heavily camouflaged and covered by a sliding hatch. There was also a remote observation post at each OB, connected to the main hideout by telephone and at which messages could be received with-out the location of the parent hideout being revealed.

Most of the hideouts were blown up as normality returned to the county, but some still remain to this day, including the following pair.

CREECH BARROW
OS: SY 939828

The remains of this hide are relatively (and only relatively!) easy to find. From Wareham follow the signs 'Blue Pool' and continue southwards past the Blue Pool tourist site for about half a mile; then, where the road swings to the right, join the bridleway on the left-hand side of the road. Continue eastward along this path - following the blue pointers - for a little over half a mile until, adjacent to a patch of bogland, you reach a wooden post with the figure '7' painted on it on a blue background. Continue across a small stream to the next blue plastic pointer and - with a bit of searching - you will find the hide on a bluff on the right-hand side of the track before the next watercourse.

LANGTON HERRING
OS: SY 622822

The Langton Herring hide was used by the Auxiliary Unit commanded by the owner of the local Manor House, Captain E. B. Sparks, and was hidden in one of the few areas of really thick woodland overlooking the Chesil Beach. Like the majority of OBs, it now lies in ruins, having been blown up and later filled in to deter youngsters from the nearby village or holiday camp from endangering themselves in the ruins.

To find the spot today, take the footpath that runs from near the Methodist Church in Langton Herring (signposted 'Fleet') to join the B3157 road near the top of the hill north of the Victoria Inn. The hide is located off the track on the left-hand side, rather nearer to the edge of the wood than to the path, some 200 yards after a very sharp and obvious bend in the path (from the Langton direction).

Corrugated iron sheeting and an abundance of brambles are today's only indications of the site of the Langton Herring Operational Base.

BLANDFORD CAMP   OS: ST 914077 (entrance)

Location: To the east of Blandford Forum (well signposted).

Records exist of the Army occupying land above the town of Blandford Forum for well over 200 years, in those far off days the troops being both foot soldiers and cavalry. The 20th century saw the camp in prominence during the First World War, with the famous Royal Naval Division - naval reservists who had acted as army units under Admiralty control - being amongst units based here. By 1920, however, virtually all signs of military activity at the camp had disappeared; the buildings were demolished and the land returned to agricultural use.

As tension mounted in Europe, the decision was made to re-activate the camp at Blandford, but with all the 1914-18 hutted accommodation having long gone, a large tented camp had to be erected as a stop-gap measure - over 100 large marquees and nearly 500 smaller tents were soon in place. During the following winter lines of huts were constructed, and these were to serve Blandford well for the war years - and some for very much longer!

During the initial build-up of our forces, as reservists and militiamen reported for duty, Blandford acted as a forming-up depot, then, as the 'Phoney War' months passed by, slipped in to the routine of a training base. However, this artificial atmosphere was not to last for long, for as the military reverses of the British Expeditionary Force and its retreat to Dunkirk led to a very real threat of inva-

The Roosevelt Memorial Garden and Monument.

sion, the Blandford Garrison was augmented by, amongst others, survivors of that debacle and became pivotal to plans for the defence of the Dorset coastline.

The camp continued to be used for battle training, for both infantrymen and artillery personnel - utilising the same rolling downlands that Kitchener's Army had used some 25 years earlier - until 1944, at which time a large portion of the camp was taken over by the US Army as a major military hospital. Additionally, an American light anti-aircraft gun battalion (the 184th) was posted in, with the task of defending the massive concentrations of troops and vehicles in the local area against low-level German air attack.

The 22nd General Hospital was completed by April 1944 and, until its closure in the autumn of 1945, was to treat nearly 20,000 casualties with, at peak times of activity, over 500 wounded arriving within a given 24-hour period. As a memento of the American presence at Blandford, and even before the war in the Far East had run its full course, a memorial park was dedicated, to which a monument was later added.

Since the war Blandford Camp has continued to play an important part in the life of the British Army, and is today the home of the Royal Corps of Signals, which has moved over recent years from its base at Catterick in Yorkshire to its new home in the Dorset countryside. A massive and ongoing building programme has resulted in most of the wartime huts and other buildings being demolished, but seven Second World War 'H Block' huts still stand near Engineers Corner, a part of the camp not open to the public.

However, visitors to the Signals Museum (see separate entry, page 156) are able to absorb the atmosphere of the camp, and also to see the Roosevelt Memorial Garden and Monument next to the car park. Occasionally the Garrison invites the local community to attend events such as Beating Retreat - something certainly not to be missed!

Second World War huts still in use in the 1990s.

BOVINGTON CAMP (ALLENBY BARRACKS)

OS: SY 833895

Location: 7 miles east of Dorchester, just to the north of Wool.

The land upon which Bovington Army Camp now stands came into Army possession at the end of the last century, initially for use as an area to be used for rifle ranges and similar military training purposes. In the years from the turn of the century until the outbreak of the Great War, Bovington slowly expanded as a greater acreage of former heath and farmland was acquired from the local gentry, and during the first two years of that war became a major infantry training base and a Command Depot.

In the autumn of 1916 Bovington was chosen to be the Tank Training Centre, the facilities where the initial tank trials had taken place being too small to meet the needs of the Army's latest strategic weaponry. Tactics evolved at Bovington were to be successful in breaking the stalemate in Northern Europe and lead to the end of the carnage of trench warfare that had already decimated the youth of our nation, as well as that of both our allies and bitterest enemies. A year after the end of the war a railway branch was

Sandhurst Block, completed in 1939 as quarters for 650 troops, is the largest single building at Bovington, and one of the very few buildings of wartime vintage still to be seen at the camp today.

laid from Wool station to the Camp (part of an embankment and a bridge support can still be seen from Wool Bridge, OS: SY 845883), but it was short-lived and taken out of service in the 1920s).

In the inter-war years Bovington consolidated its position as the home of the British Army's armoured fighting vehicle forces, evolving tactics and maintenance procedures and heavily involved in training. It was not entirely tied to the Tank Corps, though, as other formations were also based there from time to time. It was during these inter-war years that T. E. Lawrence (of Arabia), who was serving in the RTC under the name of Shaw, was fatally injured in a motorcycle accident; he died in the camp's hospital on 19 May 1935, the event commemorated by a plaque in the modern Medical Centre.

With German dreams of world domination again threatening peace in Europe, and Chamberlain's Government slowly realising the seriousness of the situation, the second half of the 1930s saw expansion at Bovington gathering momentum, and by 1939 the Royal Tank Corps Training Centre and Depot was fully committed to the task of bringing Britain's tank and armoured car units to war readiness. To co-ordinate their training the Army Armoured Fighting Vehicles School was established here in 1937, with many of those learning the skills of armoured warfare having previously been cavalry officers and men!

After the fall of France and the arrival at Bovington of large numbers of evacuees from the beaches of Dunkirk, anti-invasion preparations included the formation of a number of rapid response columns of troops and armour and the consolidation of defensive measures around the camp itself. For a while much of the training was suspended, some partially trained personnel were returned to their parent

A Centurion Mk XI tank, displayed outside the unit's Driving and Maintenance School building (visible from the main road nearby).

units and preparations to meet the Wehrmacht on a Dorset battlefield took on an overriding importance. However, the only combat turned out to be between raiding Luftwaffe aircraft and the local AA gunners.

As the war progressed, the whole range of Allied tanks passed through Bovington, from the woefully inadequate light tanks of the early war years to the Shermans and Grants of the mid-war period and the Cromwells and Pershings of the final months of hostilities. Soldiers of the Commonwealth, particularly Canadians, used the Bovington (and, of course, Lulworth) facilities as they joined other Allied forces in preparation for first the strikes against the German occupiers of North Africa, Sicily and mainland Italy, then the massive and final strike against Hitler's Fortress Europe.

In the post-war years, encompassing the Cold War and the numerous hot wars and skirmishes in which British Forces have been involved, Bovington has stayed in the forefront of armoured warfare technology and tactics. Today the Royal Armoured Corps Centre is one of the few military establishments in the country (Blandford Camp is another) that continues to expand and modernise, with its Armoured Vehicle Driver Instruction Centre being at the centre of its wide range of activities.

During the last months of 1994 an all-weather armoured vehicle cross-country training track was opened on heathland to the north of the main camp, while the Tank Repair Workshops have been civilianised, with similar facilities in other parts of the country having been closed down. At the southern end of the camp stands Stanley Barracks, so named on its completion in 1939 as a hutted accommodation complex. Today the name seems particularly apt, for a small but very important part played in the removal of the invading Argentinean forces from the Falkland Islands in 1982 was played by light armoured vehicles whose crews will almost certainly have acquired at least part of their fighting skills here in Dorset.

In addition to visiting the Tank Museum (see page 157), a visit to the Bovington area provides excellent views of modern AFVs at work, with especially good views being obtained by the Lawrence of Arabia memorial tree (OS: SY 826904) and from the minor road running past Clouds Hill towards Gallows Hill, where an information board is located.

The Modern Army: a Challenger II on the training grounds north of the main camp.

BROWNSEA ISLAND COASTAL DEFENCE GUN BATTERY

OS: SZ 029876

Location: On the eastern end of Brownsea Island, in the grounds of Brownsea Castle.

Two 4.7-inch naval guns, possibly of Turkish origin, were installed here in 1940 to guard the entrance to Poole Harbour, which was sealed off to shipping during the hours of darkness. An observation minefield in the harbour mouth was monitored from the underground gun control room, and could be activated electrically if the need ever arose. (To support the minefield, an explosives-filled surplus vessel, the *Empire Sentinel*, was moored off Brownsea to be moved into the narrows to seal off the harbour in the event of imminent invasion.) The guns were manned by between 90 and 110 men of No 347 Coastal Battery of the 554th Coastal Regiment, Royal Artillery. During the build-up to 'Overlord' an American 40 mm Bofors gun battery was located on open ground to the rear of the main battery.

Today the concrete works of the two gun positions are still clearly visible, one still showing the gun mounting ring. Two searchlight buildings remain, one in use as an informal garden shelter, and the underground control room also remains - as does just one of the brick-built support buildings. Brownsea Island is owned by the National Trust, access being gained by ferries from Poole Quay and Sandbanks; unfortunately, the main battery site is within a part of Brownsea that is not open to the public, although one of the two searchlight buildings can be seen near the landing stage, and the founda-tions of a building formerly associated with this lower searchlight can be seen in the grounds of the National Trust cafe (now in use as a hard standing) on the cafe lawn. The cafe was the Officers' Mess and the Agent's House the Sergeants' Mess.

Below **The front of one of the two 4.7-inch gun positions, atop the gun control room. Garden chairs now look out across the harbour entrance, where alert artillerymen once monitored the same stretch of water.**

Bottom **One of the searchlight buildings, now a garden shelter.**

CATTISTOCK HOME GUARD HUT

OS: ST 590996

Location: Mill Lane, a cul-de-sac in Cattistock village near the Post Office.

Like nearby Maiden Newton, the attractive village of Cattistock paid a very full part in supporting the national war effort. In addition to the Home Guard unit, there was also an Observer Corps post on Norden Hill above the village.

In the first two years of the war Cattistock played host to units from the King's Own Scottish Borderers, the Royal Sussex Regiment, the Highland Light Infantry and the Royal Artillery; for the build-up to D-Day, the Royal Sussex Regiment returned, joined by personnel from the US Army. At one time the village had no fewer than 23 Nissen huts within its boundaries; today, only that used by the volunteers of the Home Guard remains standing.

Still in good repair in the 1990s, the Home Guard hut is now used as a private storeroom.

CHICKERELL AND WYKE REGIS ROYAL ENGINEER TRAINING CAMPS

OS: SY 653773 (Wyke Camp Main Entrance);
SY 648794 (Chickerell Camp Main Entrance)

> Locations: Two separate sites made up the Royal Engineer Training Camp (RETC): the Bridging Camp, at the end of Camp Road in the Weymouth suburb of Wyke Regis, and the main accommodation camp and rifle range at Chickerell, on the B3157 Weymouth to Bridport road.

The older of the sites is that at Chickerell, which came into the Army's possession in 1915 and was used as a range and a convalescence camp for, mainly, wounded Australian soldiers from the Great War. In those days it was known as 'Montevideo Camp', and Montevideo House, still to be seen today, was its Officers' Mess. The camp at Wyke was acquired by the Army in the inter-war period and was first used in May 1928.

Throughout the Second World War both sites played an important part in the training of Allied forces: general and specialised combat training at Chickerell, and the enhancing of bridge-laying and building skills at Wyke, where pontoon and Bailey bridges were erected across the narrow waters of The Fleet (the tidal water area between Chesil Beach and the mainland) and over various obstacles on drier land.

From the spring of 1944 until the battle for Europe was won, the Chickerell Camp became a major forming-up location for American equipment awaiting shipment

The main entrance to the Bridging Camp, with Chesil Beach and Lyme Bay in the background. Note the crumbling pillbox next to the Coastal Footpath signpost on the right.

out of Weymouth and Portland to the continent - virtually all vehicles approaching the port areas from the west and northwest were directed through Chickerell.

The camps continued to be used after the war, with up to 30,000 soldiers (regulars and reservists) passing annually through the RETC in the 1970s. In 1983 the Freedom of the Borough of Weymouth and Portland was awarded to the Corps of Royal Engineers in recognition of the strong bonds between the local civic and military communities.

Today, in a very much slimmed-down Army, the camps continue to be used for combat engineering training and many of the wartime Nissen huts are still in use at both Wyke and Chickerell. Good views of the activities at Wyke can be obtained from the coastal footpath running alongside the perimeter fence and a public footpath, diverted when firing is taking place, which runs through the rifle range at Chickerell (with views northwards from it to the main domestic site and its large collection of wartime buildings).

The impressive collection of wartime buildings at Chickerell Camp.

COOMBE COTTAGE, BROADSTONE

OS: SZ 015961

Location: 124 Dunyeats Road, Broadstone, a minor road between the A349 and the B3074 Poole to Wimborne Minster and Poole to Corfe Mullen roads.

Coombe Cottage was one of an innumerable number of private houses taken over for military use by one or more of the three services during the war years. Many were smaller, those around RAF Hamworthy, for example, and a lot were larger. Few, however, could have been much prettier!

The cottage was in the hands of the Army from November 1940 until June 1941 as a Headquarters building for part of the British 5th Corps - in this case the Royal Engineers' 246th Field Company (a part of the 7th Guards Brigade). At this time the Corps was commanded by a certain Lieutenant-General Bernard Montgomery, but there is no record of him ever having visited Dunyeats Road!

As a small memento of the Army's time in occupation of this attractive cottage, a former Sapper who served here - Mr Eric Harris - presented a plaque in 1986 to the then owners of the house highlighting its place in history.

The house is, of course, now back in private ownership, but can be seen clearly from the road without being intrusive.

Only the absence of a sentry, and of sticky tape at the windows, reveals that this is a 1995 view of Coombe Cottage and not one from the darkest days of the war.

EAST WEARS COASTAL DEFENCE BATTERIES

OS: SY 699731

> Location: On the north-east side of Portland, above the southern end of the dockyard complex.

The East Wears Gun Batteries were an extension of the defences of the Verne Citadel and were completed in their current structural form in the last quarter of the 19th century, with an initial armament fit of some 20 10-inch and 9-inch muzzle-loading guns. The purpose of the batteries was to cover the approaches to Portland and its harbour from the east and south-east.

During the 20th century, particularly in association with the Great War, numerous changes were made to the weapons fit, and advances in weapons technology meant that the number of guns required to meet the batteries' tasking could be dramatically reduced; thus only two 9.2-inch guns were in service at the outbreak of hostilities in 1939. Two years later, two 90 mm guns were added at E battery to supplement the older weapons, but with the Nazi regime never embarking upon its planned invasion of Britain and German naval forces never coming close enough to Portland to be engaged by the gunners manning the East Wears Batteries, the guns were never fired in anger.

The guns were finally taken out of service in 1956, but part of the complex was used by the Flag Officer Sea Training for the training of naval personnel of many nations in activities associated with help to the civilian community. The barracks and master gunner's house still stand behind A and B batteries; the E battery site is easily accessed by following the path that runs alongside the naval cemetery (see page 129).

The A and B battery complex, still standing at East Wears but showing many signs of having been used by the Royal Navy, and its NATO allies, for 'disaster ashore' training. Note the ammunition hoist still in situ.

HAYDON PARK HOSPITAL

OS: ST 670158 (entrance)

> Location: Near the village of Haydon, 2 miles south-east of Sherborne, approached through an impressive pair of wrought iron gates.

Located in parkland immediately to the east of Sherborne Park (where 29 members of C Company of the US Army's 294th Engineer Combat Battalion were killed in an anti-tank mine explosion on 20 March 1944) was the 228th United States Army Hospital. The two establishments were completely independent, so there was no clash of Geneva Convention status due to explosives being stored and used at the 294th's camp.

Opened in 1943, the hospital had a maximum capacity of 1,100 patients, accommodated in some 24 general wards, one mental ward, one isolation ward and two wards for the treatment of a specific disease that could hardly be classified as being of a combat injury nature! There were also, of course, operating theatres, as well as laboratories, a dispensary and rehabilitation facilities - together with a 'Post Exchange', the US equivalent of the British NAAFI.

The hospital closed in December 1945, having processed nearly 23,000 casualties, then served for a while as a camp for Polish refugees before finally closing down in the early 1950s.

Now in sad decay, this Nissen Hut once housed administrative and nursing staff offices.

Today there is still enough left of the hospital to be of interest and to make a visit worthwhile. On entering the park keep straight ahead at the first junction and you will soon come across the first of the few remaining buildings, the Isolation Ward - Building 140, with its number still clearly visible painted above the doorway. On your right at the next junction you can see the Mortuary building and, beyond it (not in an area accessible to the public) the large Decontamination Centre.

Keep the Mortuary on your right-hand side and look for the footpath marker behind the modern farm building coming up on your left. The path leads you between the bases of ten of the general wards (these were for surgical cases), their bases still clearly visible in the undergrowth, until you come to the only remaining Nissen hut (note the bases of the two largest wards just before you reach it) and, opposite, the remains of the water tower.

Now you must retrace your footsteps if you are to remain on the public footpath, but before doing so leave the park through a swing gate and enjoy the view down to Sherborne Castle and its lake. It was to the south of the Castle that the mine explosion occurred (OS: ST 650159), the many casualties rapidly being brought up the hill to Haydon Park Hospital.

Building 140 - the Hospital's former Isolation Ward. The Senior Officers' Quarters and the Officers' Mess stood on the open ground to the rear of this building.

Once the Hospital Mortuary, this building now finds use as a farm store.

HOLTON HEATH LIGHT ANTI-AIRCRAFT GUN TOWERS

OS: SY 939903

Location: On open heathland due west of the Holton Heath Defence Research Agency Establishment.

One of the gun sites positioned to provide close-in LAA defence for the Royal Navy Cordite Factory, Holton Heath, these two towers, although only inches apart, were separate structures. This avoided vibration from the 40 mm Bofors gun with which one was equipped degrading the vision of the observer on the other. A second similar pair of towers, which still stand, was sited slightly further to the north, near to Sandford House, and provided flanking fire to this position.

To reach the towers take the public footpath leading away from the DRA car park opposite Gate 3 across a small wooden bridge until you reach the Admiralty boundary marker (dated 1925 and of interest in its own right); turn to the right and climb the track to the top of the hillock, where the towers are clearly visible on the skyline. The nearer tower was the observation tower, the further the gun platform.

Today only the main structure of the gun towers remains, with some railings still in situ on the platforms and the in-built concrete 'ready use ammunition' lockers still to be seen.

ILSINGTON HOUSE

OS: SY 759944

Location: In the village of Puddletown on the A35, east of Dorchester (well signposted).

17th-century Ilsington House was, in 1943, commandeered for use as the Headquarters of the American 18th Infantry Regiment, part of the 1st US Division ('The Big Red One'), a formation that had already seen action in North Africa and Sicily. The site was centrally located for the Dorset ports and combat training areas, but far enough removed from the hustle and bustle of those places to allow the staffs to work away at their detailed invasion planning in relative peace and quiet.

In addition to the occupation of the main house, personnel were billeted in the wide range of stables and outhouses, as well as in the two local pubs - the King's Arms (now demolished) and the Blue Vinney. The Motor Pool was located at the northern end of Mill Street and the unit's Post Office in a cottage in Rendal's Row. The old village hall was the site of the NAAFI and the centre of most social activity.

On D-Day the 18th Infantry Regiment was to land on Omaha Beach - to be known thereafter as 'Bloody Omaha' - and suffered severe casualties in the desperate fight to get away from the shoreline and establish a defendable beach-head. Only by acts of extreme bravery - and the German Command's indecision on the use of its armoured reserves - did they manage to gain the necessary foothold for later advance into the boscage countryside of Normandy. Later in the campaign the Regiment's Commanding Officer, Colonel George Smith, was amongst those killed in action.

Today this fine and beautifully maintained mansion is back in private ownership. The house (Tel: 01305-848454), together with its 6 acres of landscaped gardens, is open to the public:

May to September (except August): Wednesdays and Thursdays, 2.00 to 6.00 pm
August: Wednesdays, Thursdays, Sundays and Bank Holidays, 2.00 to 6.00 pm.

The south side of Ilsington House, basking in summer sunshine. Did the resident American personnel, I wonder, play croquet?

KINGSTON LACY HOUSE   OS: ST 978014

Location: On the B3082 Wimborne
Minster to Blandford Forum road.

The 106th United States General
Hospital was one of five general hospitals
built in Dorset and ready to receive casualties by the spring of 1944. The Kingston
Lacy Hospital, located in open parkland
to the east of the stately Kingston Lacy
House, had facilities to cope with up to
1,248 sick and wounded, with an over-
load capacity of 1,462. It was staffed by
between 60 and 70 doctors, more than
100 nurses and over 500 support personnel; the majority of the accommodation
was in some 90-plus wooden huts, which
had brick plinths and concrete bases, but
on occasions some tentage was also
utilised. In general the most serious casualties were treated at nearby Blandford at
the US 131st General Hospital, and the
106th dealt with the less seriously wounded and those established on the road to
recovery.

The hospital continued to receive casualties, both from US forces in the local
area and from the battlefields of Europe,
until the end of the war, finally closing in
1947. The buildings were used for a variety of purposes in the post-war years,
including use by the British Army, the
housing of displaced Yugoslavians who
had supported the German cause and,
later, for visitors to the area taking working farm holidays. To utilise their labour
in local road repairs, some German

**The last remaining ward today. The lettering
referred to in the text is on the far end of the
hut, as seen from this angle.**

POWs were housed at Kingston Lacy, in a small camp below St Stephen's church.

Today Kingston Lacy House and its surrounding grounds are in the ownership of the National Trust, and are open to the public from spring to autumn at well-publicised times. Of the wartime hospital, in addition to some roadways three major artifacts remain: a brick building, which was the Ambulance Garage, the maintenance ramp from the Motor Transportation Pool and, most interestingly, just one of the hospital wards. This latter building is now in use as a National Trust Base Camp for volunteers working on the estate - and on the wall at the north end of the hut can still be seen, in white paint on the brick background, the markings 'ISOLATION WARD - 10 BED'!

These three structures are to the east of the house and outside the area of the estate normally open to the public; however, the old ward can be seen from the Deliveries & Staff Entrance off the minor road past St Stephen's church, and the other two from the second (private) entrance to the estate when approaching Kingston Lacey from the Wimborne direction. Distant views of the two buildings can be obtained by walking along the path running eastward in front of the house until reaching the kissing gate with a 'Private' sign on it. Finally, note that the flat area immediately in front of the house is where a Halifax aircraft of No 58 Squadron, based at RAF Holmsley South, crashed on 24 January 1943, killing all of the crew.

The Motor Transportation Pool's maintenance ramp. The Ambulance Garage still stands, in a well-tended condition, to the left of this ramp.

LULWORTH ARMY CAMP AND GUNNERY RANGES

OS: SY 835816
(Main Camp Entrance)

After elements of the newly formed Tank Corps moved to Bovington Camp in November 1916, land was obtained early the following year at Lulworth to allow a live firing danger area for the unit to be established nearby. Additional land was obtained in 1918 and in February of that year the Lulworth Gunnery School was established and, despite the general rundown of the armed forces in the 1920s and 1930s, the base flourished in the inter-war years and the training facilities were regularly updated.

When war came to Europe for the second time in 25 years, the Lulworth facilities were rapidly expanded to cope with the influx of regular and reserve forces personnel who were to fight in the newly

warranted Royal Armoured Corps. Following the fall of France in June 1940, and the miracle of Dunkirk, the facilities were put under extreme pressure as all the stops were pulled out to ready the nation to combat the anticipated Nazi invasion of Britain. As the war progressed and American Lend Lease equipment became available in the form of Grant, Lee and Sherman tanks, plus the British-built Churchills and Cromwells, the range area was expanded to allow high-velocity live firing to take place under realistic conditions. Much of the credit for the success

The impressive pre-war Officers' Mess at Lulworth, itself enjoying glorious views southwards towards the coastline.

of Allied armoured forces in the Second World War, often fighting in tanks lacking in the gun power of their adversaries, can quite fairly be claimed by the staff of the Lulworth Gunnery School.

With the end of the war, despite some vocal opposition, the Army retained the range areas - which have a 6.5-mile fore-shore length - and for the last 50 years they have been used to provide training facilities for the most modern of armoured fighting vehicles. Almost all of the old wooden-hutted accommodation has been replaced by modern buildings; however, the attractive Officers' Mess was in use during the war, and remains today as an historic tribute to the leadership and bravery that has been moulded over the years at this important Army base.

Today Lulworth Camp is parented by Bovington, but remains an integral part of the British Army's training machine. The ranges walks are open to the public at most weekends, over public holidays and during the whole of August each year, and are a haven for wildlife and blessed with some of the finest coastal scenery any-where in the British Isles. At the public viewpoint between Lulworth Camp and the grounds of Lulworth Castle (on the B3070 at OS: SY 845818) one can watch in safety today's army firing its latest weaponry, including the impressive Challenger II main battle tank.

Just to the east of the viewpoint, and on the other side of the road, note the two breaks in the estate wall; these were the entrances to 'Park Camp', a training and accommodation camp in the grounds of Lulworth Castle for American personnel prior to D-Day.

With the dip in the cliffs at Arish Mell Gap in the background, a pair of Challenger I tanks fire southwards over the RAC Gunnery Ranges (as seen from the public viewpoint).

Above Built on classic architectural lines, these 1930s buildings were in use during the Second World War for classroom instruction of soldiers in training at Lulworth Ranges, and now find similar use as accommodation for simulators and other training aids used to bring the modern soldier to the peak of fighting efficiency.

Below This, one of the very few wooden buildings left at Lulworth, houses the Gunnery School Headquarters.

LYME REGIS COASTAL DEFENCE GUN BATTERY

OS: SY 346933

> Location: On 'The Spittles' National Trust land, off Timber Hill and adjacent to the Lyme Regis Golf Club.

The Timber Hill 376 Coastal Defence Battery RA above Lyme Regis, on the old packhorse road to Charmouth and beyond, was one of the 'Emergency Gun Batteries' set up on the Dorset coastline when the threat of invasion from across the Channel was very real, and consisted of two 4.7-inch naval guns (range approximately 6 miles) removed from a Great War destroyer, two searchlights and a pair of Lewis guns for point AA defence; the heavy guns had an excellent field of fire out over the waters of Lyme Bay. Great efforts were made to hide and camouflage the site, with the magazines being buried deep underground and the above-ground structures that were not set back in the pine trees having their real identities masked by being painted as farm buildings.

With the risk of invasion virtually over, the guns were removed in 1943 and the site was handed over to the US Army. Thus they were not operational when, maybe, they could have opened fire against the German E-boats attacking the Exercise 'Tiger' Force on the night of 27 April 1944. Such are the fortunes of war!

Today only four support building bases and a set of stone steps give any indication of the site's existence, for in recent years the major portion of the battery has, sadly, slipped seawards in a series of cliff falls and been lost from sight for ever. A limited amount of car parking space is available by the entrance gate to 'The Spittles'; start looking for artifacts on your left-hand side as you reach the coastal footpath direction sign.

Steps leading off the modern Dorset Coast Path indicate where one of the site's support buildings was located.

This is where the guns once stood covering Lyme Bay. Now the gun pits themselves are covered - with glutinous clay!

MAIDEN NEWTON VILLAGE

OS: SY 596977 (village centre)

> Location: Maiden Newton is located on the A356, Dorchester to Crewkerne road.

There is a fascinating collection of Second World War memorabilia within the village of Maiden Newton, much of it chronicled by the Maiden Newton & District Community Museum Trust.

Throughout the war years there was an Army presence in the village, units of the Lincolnshire Regiment being the first to arrive in 1939 and, of course, the American Army being there in strength in 1943 and 1944. As in so many of the county's southern villages, the lanes, woods and fields around Maiden Newton were filled to bursting point with vehicles and equipment prior to D-Day.

A gun emplacement, manned it is said by French Canadians, was located near to the school annex in Chilfrome Lane, with a field of fire towards West Bay - a possible beach assault landing site. The railway line from West Bay was considered a possible route inland for the enemy and large numbers of Dragon's Teeth were installed to funnel armoured vehicles towards kill zones. Many properties in the village were commandeered, with Maiden Newton House, near the church, used as a Headquarters and Officers' Mess.

Amongst the artifacts left to be seen today are the following:

Two lines of a total of 51 Dragon's Teeth

on the disused railway line off Chilfrome Lane.

Nissen huts in Chilfrome Lane.

Remains of an ammunition store in the field almost opposite the mill (approached via a small bridge on a public footpath).

Bullet hole from a strafing Heinkel in the west window of the church.

'Dragon's Teeth' and a defensive pillbox on the Yeovil to Dorchester West railway line, to the south of Maiden Newton station.

Pillbox and Dragon's Teeth to the south of the railway station (visible from the station yard or the end of Bull Lane).

Dragon's Teeth, well overgrown, between Cattistock Road and the River Frome.

A former Army Nissen hut in Chilfrome Lane, with Maiden Newton House visible in the distance.

NOTHE FORT, WEYMOUTH

OS: SY 687787

> Location: On the south side of Weymouth Harbour (well signposted).

The wall plaque commemorating the 104th Heavy Anti-Aircraft Battery's association with the Nothe is on the right-hand side as you pass through the tunnel.

The Nothe Fort was completed and commissioned in 1872 at a cost of £120,000, and played a not insignificant role during the 1939-45 war when its main armament consisted of three 6-foot breech-loading and two 6-pound quick-firing guns optimised in the coastal defence role. Point anti-aircraft defence was initially provided by a Vickers Pom Pom gun, and later by the ubiquitous 40 mm Bofors. The fort's underground magazines housed the local central ammunition depot, and on the glacis to the rear of the fort (now a car

The fort entrance with the 40 mm Bofors gun above.

park) a battery of 3.7-inch guns provided AA defence for the Weymouth and Portland Harbour areas.

Only these latter guns, and the lighter AA weapons, saw regular action; however, during July 1940 the 6-inch guns opened fire 'across the bows' of two unidentified ships entering Weymouth Bay. A hasty exchange of signals showed them to be carrying refugees from the Channel Islands!

The concept of coastal defence from fixed gun batteries was abandoned in 1956 and the guns were taken away for scrap; the fort was sold to Weymouth Borough Council six years later. Then in 1979 the Weymouth Civic Society obtained a licence to restore the fort and open it to the public.

Today this impressive fortress houses the Museum of Coastal Defence (see Museums section, page 154), covering a span of time much greater than the Second World War period - although 1939 to 1945 is, of course, very well represented.

The sheer bulk of the fort is best appreciated when viewed from seawards, or from the end of Weymouth's Stone Pier. Just visible beyond the railings is a later-period pillbox.

Gun positions on the battlements, with the re-installed 6-inch naval gun clearly visible. This photograph alone indicates how well Weymouth Bay, with its safe anchorage, was covered from the Nothe.

PARNHAM HOUSE

OS: ST 475003

> Location: On the A3066 road, three-quarters of a mile south of Beaminster.

Beautiful Parnham House, well over 300 years old, was requisitioned for use by British Army units in the early days of the war and saw service for a short while as a military hospital. From the end of 1942 until mid-1943 there was virtually no military presence at the house, but this then changed dramatically when, under the command of Colonel G. A. Taylor, the Regimental Command Post for the 16th Infantry Regiment was established here - with units billeted as far away as Lyme Regis, Abbotsbury and Litton Cheney, as well as in hutted and tented accommodation within the grounds.

Much of the detailed planning for the assault on Omaha Beach was carried out in the house's stately rooms, while outside vast amounts of armoured fighting vehicles were assembled in local fields and lanes prior to being moved on towards the coast. With a foothold in France established, the American presence reduced to zero, and Parnham's last significant military usage was as a German prisoner-of-war camp.

Today the house is open to the public - although no traces remain of its wartime use - and can be visited between April and October on Wednesdays, Saturdays, Sundays and Bank Holidays from 10.00 am to 5.00 pm.

(See also Rhodes-Moorhouse Memorial, page 140.)

At peace: Parnham House today shows no obvious signs of its military use during the Second World War.

PEVERILL POINT GUN EMPLACEMENT

OS: SZ 040786

> Location: The headland at the extreme south-east corner of Swanage Bay, sign-posted 'Peverill Point' from near the pier and also from the adjacent large car park.

Two 4-inch calibre guns, of naval origin, were located at Peverill Point to provide enfilading fire northwards across Swanage Bay; their limit of traverse was such that they could not fire directly to seaward or to the south across Durlston Bay. Located below the main guns, at the water's edge, was a third position, which presumably mounted lighter weapons. The battery was manned by members of the local Home Guard unit.

Today all three structures continue to serve useful purposes. The one in the lower position and one of the two above it are in use as shelters for those strolling along this attractive headland and wishing to pause awhile to enjoy the sea views, while the third is in use as a lookout station for HM Coastguard - an excellent example of converting a structure of war to one of peace!

When proceeding from the town out to Peverill Point, note **Swanage Pier**. As an anti-invasion measure the landward end of the pier was blown up during the days of the war when an enemy landing seemed almost imminent, and today it is easy to see where the necessary repairs to restore the pier were carried out - the concrete supports are the replacement post-war ones.

One of the Peverill Point gun positions, viewed from the roof of another, with Swanage Pier in the background.

PIDDLEHINTON CAMP

OS: SY 721965

Location: Alongside the B3143 road,
south of Piddlehinton village.

Land for an army base at Piddlehinton was requisitioned by the War Department from local farmer Phillip Tory in 1937 and work on a hutted camp started immediately. An offer of the land back for agricultural use after the war was not taken up by the farmer.

Piddlehinton Camp saw a great variety of units passing through or in residence during the war years, among the first being elements of the 4th Battalion of the Northumberland Fusiliers, who were brought here after their gallant action at Dunkirk. After only a short while they were assigned to coastal defence duties in anticipation of Hitler's invasion of mainland Britain.

In the months leading up to 'Overlord' the camp was a main base, assigned the code 'D6', for elements of the 1st US Army, including the 18th and 26th Infantry Regiments, Divisional Artillery, 1st Medical Battalion and 1st Division US Military Police. Additionally, just prior to D-Day itself, troop formations moved here from Devon before their final move to the ports of Portland and Weymouth for embarkation.

Later in the summer of 1944 troops of the US 99th Infantry Division were based here - and entered the pages of history as a result of their brave action against overwhelming odds, and without air support because of poor weather, in holding up the German advance through the

The old Main Guardroom, now converted to a private residence bearing the name 'The Easters'.

Ardennes Forest in 'The Battle of the Bulge'.

One of the saddest incidents of the war involved troops who had been quartered at Piddlehinton Camp, for it was on Christmas Day 1944, when their thoughts would have been with loved ones far away, that over 800 US Army personnel were drowned off Cherbourg, when the troopship *Leopoldville* was sent to the bottom by a German U-boat.

In post-war years Piddlehinton Camp was used as a training camp for both regular and territorial forces, and after being used to house Asian refugees from Uganda in 1972, was finally given up by the Army in the mid-1970s (but with a small corner being retained for occasional use to this day). The rest of the site was acquired by Dorset County Council in November 1979, which converted some of the larger buildings into business units and set aside the hutted accommodation for homeless families.

Today access to the former camp roads is unrestricted and good views can easily be obtained of the many huts and buildings left from army days. Although there is rather a run-down air about the place, it takes very little imagination to envisage what it was like here in busy former years.

Now leased by the Dorchester Rifle Club, the old butts continue in use as a shooting range.

PILLBOXES AND ANTI-TANK OBSTACLES

Driving or walking around the Dorset countryside one could be excused for thinking that the Second World War pillboxes and anti-tank obstacles still to be seen today are merely 'just scattered about'; this is, however, generally not the case. The pillboxes, or 'strong posts' as they were officially known, and anti-tank obstacles formed part of a series of national 'stop lines' designed to hinder a German advance inland from a landing on the South Coast.

In Dorset one stop line was on the coast itself and the second ran along the valley of the River Frome from the Maiden Newton area to the western shores of Poole Harbour. Individual pillboxes were also positioned to protect vital installations such as airfields, ports and the Royal Navy Cordite Factory at Holton Heath.

I have listed here but a representative few of the many still to be seen in the county today.

BLANDFORD FORUM

OS: ST 885065 (town centre)

Even the most casual of observers could hardly fail to notice that the attractive Georgian town of Blandford has more than the usual number of Dragon's Teeth and pillboxes within its boundaries; some may even wonder why?

Should a Nazi invasion of Dorset, by seaborne or airborne forces, ever have been attempted, Blandford Forum would have played a major part in attempts to prevent the invading forces from moving inland to

establish a major bridgehead, for in 1940 it was configured as an official Anti-Tank Island. The natural defensive features of the River Stour and the man-made ones of the embankments and deep cuttings of the Somerset & Dorset Railway's line were supplemented by pillboxes, extensive Dragon's Teeth and, to the north of Crown Meadows, a high anti-tank ditch. It was hoped that the German forces could be channelled away from the town itself,

Anti-tank devices located behind the boundary wall of Blandford's Crown Hotel.

The anti-tank ditch, with defensive pillbox, on the north side of Crown Meadows. The ditch served two purposes: to act purely as an obstacle, and to expose to anti-tank weapons fire the poorly armoured underside of any fighting vehicle trying to scale it.

out to an area upon which artillery was already zeroed-in, and face annihilation.

The passing of over 50 years has seen many of the fortifications removed or demolished, and since 1966 the trains of the S&D no longer make their way through Blandford *en route* for either Bournemouth West or Bath, but today much still remains. Perhaps the easiest way to see a representative selection is by viewing the Dragon's Teeth near to, and in the grounds of, the Crown Hotel, and the anti-tank ditch, with pillbox, in nearby Crown Meadows (not to be confused with the flood defence embankment nearer to the river). Note also, in the Hotel garden wall, the dummy pillbox firing apertures. Crown Meadows and the Crown Hotel are on your left-hand side when entering the town from the south across the River Stour.

Further Dragon's Teeth can be seen in the Langton Street car park, off East Street, as can the last vestiges of the old S&D embankment. The Scout Hut off Bryanstone Street was used as the local Home Guard Headquarters.

HOLTON HEATH

OS: SY 952920

Location: On the south side of the A351 road, at its junction with a private road leading to East Holton Farm, near to the Romany Centre.

This small pillbox was an integral part of the defences of the Royal Navy Cordite Factory. In daily use, however, it was used as the control point for traffic and personnel wishing to pass along the main

The Holton Heath pillbox.

road alongside the factory, for this road was closed to civilians during the war and access totally prohibited to non-passhold-ers. The equivalent position at the western end of the RNCF site has been demolished.

MORETON

> Location: On the north side of the ford and footbridge across the River Frome, near St Nicholas's church in the village of Moreton.

A round, concrete pillbox, with brickwork base and roof, was sited to cover a crossing of the River Frome. It is unusual for such a small pillbox in having seven firing positions; it also has a very small and low access hatch.

(Although beyond the scope of this book, the church at Moreton merits a mention: it received extensive bomb damage on 8 October 1940 and the replacement etched windows by Lawrence Whistler, installed in 1955 and one of

Moreton pillbox.

which shows a Spitfire in flight, are truly beautiful and well worth viewing.)

POOLE TOWN

> Location: Tatnam Farm Allotments, off Wimborne Road or Sherrin Close, Poole, to the rear of St Mary's Roman Catholic Church.

Over 30 Dragon's Teeth obstacles remain in situ here: four in the church grounds, with six fallen and over 20 still upright in the allotment area (which drains into an old anti-tank ditch). Poole, like Blandford Forum, was a designated Anti-Tank Island, these obstacles being part of its structure, with a minefield having been laid nearby.

The Poole Dragon's Teeth.

Another view of the Poole Dragon's Teeth.

SEACOMBE CLIFF

OS: SY 985767

Location: On the Dorset Coast Path to the west of St Aldhelm's Head, most easily accessed by the public footpath running coastward from Acton village, via Eastington Farm. It is on your left-hand side, set back from the path on the hillside, as you approach the cliff edge from the north.

This was an Alan-Williams turret in a particularly remote location. It was a brave man, regular soldier or member of the Home Guard, who manned this position alone on a windswept night, particularly at the height of the 1940 invasion scare! The turret is in rather better condition than the one by Worbarrow Tout (see page 69).

SEATOWN BEACH

OS: SY 420917

Location: To the east of the stream joining the sea at Seatown Beach, approached by an unclassified road from the village of Chideock.

Some 50-plus years after being positioned as part of the anti-invasion defences, the Dragon's Teeth at Seatown have gradually succumbed to successive West Bay gales and storms.

Dragon's Teeth on Seatown Beach.

STERTE ROAD, POOLE

OS: SZ 011919

Location: The west side of Sterte Road, where it crosses the Weymouth to Poole railway line.

This Type 22 pillbox, manufactured from a combination of bricks and concrete and aligned to face to the north, was part of the defensive chain around the town of Poole, with its important harbour and industrial facilities. Now covered in ivy and brambles, it remains in good structural condition, nestling in the approach road embankment at the Sterte Road railway overbridge. It is best viewed from the small industrial estate below.

The pillbox in Sterte Road, Poole.

SWANAGE SEAFRONT

OS: SZ 030793

Location: In public gardens on the seafront on the road out of Swanage towards Studland.

This defensive strong point was located to give direct fire across Swanage Bay from a slightly elevated position behind the seafront (itself lying behind reams of barbed wire and other defensive structures on the foreshore). Access to the gun position was from the rear, through a partially underground secondary structure.

Today the main structure has a much more peaceful *raison d'être*, being in use as a shelter, with benches, in the attractive gardens that grace Swanage's seafront - and from which, on a clear day, magnificent views can be enjoyed to the Needles and Isle of Wight beyond. Now those who look seaward from here will have quite different thoughts in their minds from

The former defensive strong point on the seafront at Swanage.

those who did so more than 50 years ago when invasion was expected by troops of the Wehrmacht and it was felt - at least by some - that it was only a matter of time before landing barges would loom over the horizon!

WAREHAM TOWN

OS: SY 923878

Location: Built into the wall below
St Martin's church at the northern end of
North Street.

This strong point was sited to cover the main approach to the town of Wareham from the direction of the River Piddle valley and the main railway line. The position was entered via a set of brick steps leading down from the churchyard and originally had two firing windows; today, however, one of the apertures has been concreted over and only the one facing North Street remains open. Although easy to see if pointed in the right direction, the structure blends in with other stonework in the area and was thus well camouflaged.

(Note at the other end of the town, adjacent to the library, the D-Day 50th Anniversary plaque.)

The well-camouflaged strong point in North Street, Wareham.

WEST STAFFORD

OS: SY 723901

Location: At the junction of the minor
roads from West Stafford and from
Lower Bockhampton to Dorchester.

The West Stafford pillbox.

This Type 22 pillbox was located on the Maiden Newton to Poole Harbour 'Stop Line' and positioned in the valley of the River Frome. It remains in good condition and can be clearly seen from the roadway nearby.

WOODSFORD CASTLE

OS: SY 758904

> Location: In the grounds of Woodsford Castle, on a minor road 4 miles east of Dorchester.

What is now known as Woodsford Castle, and in the ownership of the Landmark Trust, is actually the only remaining side of a small quadrangular castle built here in the Frome Valley in the middle of the 14th century - and unique in being thatched!

The pillbox, which is of interest to us in the period at which we are looking, is a four-sided brick structure with a concrete roof, which possesses three firing apertures and is orientated towards the south and designed, presumably, to offer fire to an enemy advancing northwards towards the Frome Valley from the direction of Warmwell airfield.

The Castle is not open to the public (but can be rented for holidays from the

Pillbox and castle - a contrast in defensive philosophies!

Landmark Trust, tel 01225 705676); however, the pillbox is easily visible from the passing road and makes an interesting comparison with the remains of the fortifications of some 600 years ago.

WORBARROW BAY

OS: SY 872797

> Location: On the right-hand side of the footpath leading from the Tyneham village car park to the sea at Worbarrow Tout, just a hundred yards or so back from the shoreline.

This defensive position took the form of an Alan-Williams steel turret, rather reminiscent of the cupolas atop the Maginot Line! The top of the turret rotated on a series of wheels about the base and could be fitted for a range of light weapons such as the Bren gun or the Boys anti-tank rifle. Today the turret bears the scars of Lulworth Range activities - at least two 30

The Alan-Williams turret at Worbarrow Bay.

mm cannon holes and one from a larger-calibre weapon - but the rotating apparatus is still in situ, together with the gun mounting.

WORBARROW BAY DRAGON'S TEETH

OS: SY 872796

> Location: On the east side of Worbarrow Tout, near Tyneham village.

This set of concrete Dragon's Teeth anti-tank obstacles was constructed to completely block the way off the beach on the eastern side of the Worbarrow Tout coastal feature, thus forcing any amphibious fighting vehicles to land on the more open beaches of Worbarrow Bay itself - tactically much less suitable, as it was covered by a number of well-positioned strong points.

Dragon's Teeth at Worbarrow Bay.

PORTLAND HEAVY ANTI-AIRCRAFT GUN BATTERY

OS: SY 693731

> Location: On open ground directly to the south of Priory Road, which runs past the RN Memorial and the Portland Heights Hotel towards the Verne.
> A public footpath passes close by the site.

Having excellent arcs of fire over the harbour and southwards towards enemy-occupied France, from whence the main threat came, the Portland (or Verne) HAA site - one up to of 30 heavy anti-aircraft gun sites within the county at any one time - was fitted with six 3.7-inch guns manned by personnel of AA Command. The initial fit had been of four guns, replacing a battery of obsolescent 3-inch guns sited on the glacis of the Verne Citadel (see separate entry, page 85). The associated Gun Operations Room (GOR) was at Red Barracks, Weymouth, then later at Nottington House, Weymouth (now demolished). As the war progressed, the site was updated with state-of-the-art electronic predictors and radar control.

On the subject of radar, note near Priory Corner (the sharp bend overlooking Chesil Beach on the road up to the top of Portland at OS: SY 685728) the few remains of the **RAF Westcliff** radar unit: two sets of concrete steps with iron railings, and some demolished building ruins in the chasm between the two flat areas of ground to which they lead. The unit functioned from May 1942 until the early post-war years.

Today the HAA site is occupied by Newground Stables. The concrete works are clearly visible, being gun pits and ready-use ammunition lockers; additionally, some of the old perimeter fence posts remain standing.

One of the gun pits, now used for feeding the resident horses.

Horses peacefully graze where the noise would have been overpowering on the many occasions when the Portland HAA battery was in action against enemy raiders.

POUNDBURY BARRACKS, DORCHESTER

OS: SY 688907

Location: Bridport Road, Top o' Town, Dorchester.

The Barracks here was completed in the 1790s, the impressive Keep being added in 1879 as an Armourer's Stores. The Dorsetshire Regiment established its Depot at Poundbury in 1881.

During the First World War the Depot served the usual functions of such a facility in providing a firm base for the infantry regiment's battalions while they were abroad, including the very important task of encouraging men of Dorset to rally to the colours.

This continued in the inter-war years,

until the threat of hostilities again saw Dorchester's Barracks a hive of activity as the Regiment's two regular battalions and one, then a second, battalion of Territorials were prepared for war. The initial four battalions rose to nine, with the Regiment seeing service in France, Malta, Sicily and Italy, Burma and in North West Europe from Normandy to the Baltic. Basic training was carried out at the Depot and in the local area, before personnel were sent off to join their individual battalions. Also in residence here for a time were members of No 47 Royal

The Keep, with the part of the former Army Depot complex now in use as a Post Office Sorting Office visible on the right.

Marine Commando, whose D-Day task was to be the capture of Port-en-Bessin, with its small - but strategic - harbour located between Gold and Omaha assault beaches.

In the autumn of 1943 parts of the Barracks were taken over by the US Army, and together with a temporary camp off Poundbury Road (which runs alongside the Keep) was designated as camp 'D7'. The 701st Ordnance Maintenance Company and the 1st Quartermasters Company were the new residents, the 701st's No 3 Platoon being accommodated in the Barracks and their colleagues in the nearby huts and tents. As the Americans embarked for Normandy, the US presence dramatically reduced, but the Depot continued its pivotal function of supporting the Dorsets, both in Europe and in the 'Forgotten Army' in the Far East.

In one of the many British Forces cut-backs of the second half of the 20th century the Regiment lost its individual identity when, on 21 May 1958, it was amalgamated with the Devonshire Regiment to form the Devonshire & Dorset Regiment.

In March 1960 it was announced that the Dorchester Barracks was surplus to Ministry of Defence requirements and all but a small part of the complex was sold off. Today the Keep houses an excellent military museum (see separate entry, page 155) and the Post Office and Dorset County Council own the majority of the remaining old and historic buildings. The Army still has a presence, however, the local Territorial Unit being based adjacent to the Keep in Poundbury Road. Of recent interest was the impressive parade held here on 30 July 1994 to commemorate the Barracks' 200th Anniversary.

Once the RSM's hallowed ground, the parade square is now a car park!

RED (OR WEYMOUTH) BARRACKS

OS: SY 682786

> Location: Horsford Road, Weymouth
> (near the Nothe Gardens and Fort and
> high above Weymouth Harbour).

The only remaining one of three barracks built in Weymouth and Melcombe Regis during the 18th century, when the resort was achieving fame as the bathing station of King George III, this particular barracks complex was completed in 1795, at the time of Napoleon Bonaparte's rise to power. Built as a cavalry barracks, following a disastrous fire it was rebuilt as an infantry barracks in 1801.

Its initial use in the Second World War was from 1939 to 1941 as the Gun Operations Room controlling the anti-aircraft gun sites for the whole of the county of Dorset. However, in 1941 the county's AA defence co-ordination was divided between two GORs, one at Nottington House, Weymouth, and the other at South Lytchett Manor, near Poole. From this time until the end of the war, Red Barracks (as it was always locally known) was used for troop accommodation, especially for Royal Artillery personnel manning local gun and searchlight batteries and for Royal

The elegance of the conversion to residential units of the former barracks buildings shows to good advantage is this view from the highway outside. The small building to the left of the entrance was once the armoury; that to the right (behind the 'Wellington Court' sign) was the guardroom.

Engineers supporting them, and for administrative support.

The barracks were very little used after the return of peace to our island in 1945 - just occasional visits by Territorial Army units and other minor utilisation - and gradually began to look the worse for wear. Luckily, in 1964 and before the decay became too bad, the Post Office bought the site from the Ministry of Defence and used it mainly as a sorting office until 1975 - after which it lay empty (and again started to deteriorate). There was much local controversy when plans were announced to demolish the barracks, which occupy a commanding position on the Weymouth skyline, and only the intervention of the Secretary of State for the Environment at the time (Mr Peter Shore) stopped such a thoughtless course of action being taken.

The site was eventually sold in 1981 and now, as Wellington Court, boasts a fine conversion to 72 units of residential accommodation, while still retaining much of the character of a barracks of the 18th and 19th centuries.

Directly opposite the entrance to Wellington Court lies **Bincleaves Barracks**, which was the Headquarters for Fortress Dorset until 1941, when the county fortress concept of defence was abandoned. Until recently it continued to serve as a Territorial Army base, but now 'Options for Change' has led to that no longer being the case. Today the site of Bincleaves Barracks is the base of the local Army and Sea Cadet units, the Weymouth Squadron (No 1606) of the Air Training Corps, and in addition a nationally important Sea Cadet Corps Training Centre has been established there.

Unmistakably of a military design, two more of the old buildings show the tasteful way in which the conversion of Red Barracks to Wellington Court was carried out.

RIVER LYDDEN BRIDGE

OS: ST 751137

Location: On the A357 road between Sturminster Newton and Shepton Mallet, at the village of Bagber.

This bridge, known locally as Twofords Bridge, was erected by engineers of the US Army during the build-up to Operation 'Overlord', as it was considered that the old stone bridge across the River Lydden was too weak for heavy vehicles, such as tank transporters, as they made their way in the early summer of 1944 towards the embarkation ports of Weymouth and Portland. The military bridge was built directly alongside its much older counterpart.

Today both bridges remain, the newer one carrying eastbound traffic. As part of the county's D-Day 50th Anniversary Commemorations, Dorset County Council erected a plaque on the girder bridge in 1994. It reads: 'D-Day 6th June. 50th Anniversary 1944-1994. Dorset County Council'.

The old and the (relatively) new, viewed along the A357 towards Sturminster Newton. Note to the left of the fourth upright girder on the far side the plaque mentioned in the text.

SOUTH LYTCHETT MANOR

OS: SY 959935

> Location: Post Green Road, Lychett Minster - lying in parkland off the B3067.

18th-century South Lychett Manor, no longer a private house in 1941 but a girls' boarding school, was requisitioned at that time for Army use and became the East Dorset Gun Operations Room (GOR) for the co-ordination of the AA defence of East Dorset; at the same time the West Dorset GOR was established at Nottington House, Weymouth - now demolished. (Previously the Red Barracks GOR had covered the whole county.)

Although communication between the gun sites and the GORs was normally by land line, back-up radio circuits were established and the roof of the house was fitted with two 35-foot masts; otherwise, except for a new entrance door (still in use), there were no real external signs of the building's conversion to operational use. Internally, of course, many changes were made, the most important being the conversion of the room adjacent to the entrance lobby to the Sector Operations Room. The house ceased to be a GOR in 1944.

Today this attractive house is once more a school - now Lychett Minster Upper School, a state school within the Dorset Education System and with an excellent academic record. The old house can be seen from local minor roads and from the dual carriageway (A35) running into Poole from the west.

The west face of the house, with school pupils and civilian cars instead of troops and military vehicles in the foreground. The Sector Operations Room was in the room directly behind the white Volvo; the Radio Room on the first floor behind the F-registered Fiesta and the Signals Workshop to the left of the white entrance door.

STUDLAND BAY

OS: SZ 039825
(National Trust Middle Beach car park)

> Location: Studland Bay lies at the easternmost end of the Purbeck Hills, with Old Harry Rocks marking its southern extremity and the entrance to Poole Harbour its northern one.

Wartime artifacts in the area around beautiful Studland Bay can be readily divided into two categories: those associated with defence in the darkest days of the war, and those associated with training and preparation for the Allies' return to mainland Europe - and ultimate victory.

The British General Staff considered the sandy stretch of Studland's beach one of the probable sites that would have been selected for the landing of troops if Hitler's planned invasion of England (Operation 'Sealion') had gone ahead, so the coastline was relatively well defended - mainly by conventional pillboxes and anti-tank devices, but also by a scheme to set the sea alight with burning oil. Known as Project Fougasse, the scheme consisted of a series of pipes laid just offshore and a system to ignite them as the enemy's

seaborne forces approached. It was, however, vulnerable to the vagaries of wind and tide, and a night-time practice burn for the GOC Southern Command and his senior officers on 20 December 1940 had to be abandoned, although an earlier one in the day had been considered a success.

As the fortunes of war slowly changed in the Allies' favour, Studland Bay became a major training ground for the troops, sailors and airmen who would lead the assault on Fortress Europe, and a whole range of exercises, of increasing complexity, were held here - culminating in Exercise 'Smash III' held in mid-April 1944, when Prime Minister Churchill and Generals Eisenhower and Montgomery were among those observing the practice landings from the shelter of the specially built observation bunker known as Fort Henry (built by Canadian engineers in 1943). The 1st Battalion of the Dorsetshire Regiment, who would be amongst the first to land on Gold Beach on D-Day, were fully involved - like all other participants, experiencing live ammunition being used as an integral part

Keeping the sea and not the Germans at bay! Dragon's Teeth on the beach at Studland, now serving as sea defences.

Above **Project Fougasse pumping station in the grounds opposite the Knoll House Hotel.**

Below **The massive Fort Henry above Redend Point, behind the far end of which is a defensive gun position from earlier in the war.**

of the exercise. (Signs warning of the risk of unexploded live ammunition remained in place here until well into the 1950s.)

There is much of interest still to be seen at Studland Bay today, perhaps the best way being to park at, or walk to, the National Trust's Middle Beach car park in Studland village, and start from there. Some 16 Dragon's Teeth anti-tank obstacles, most still standing and many covered in ivy, can be found on leaving the parking area by the steps at the far side from the entrance and walking behind the old coastguard station and beach huts until reaching a small gully, where they will be seen in the trees on your left.

Backtrack along the beach towards Redend Point and you will see other Dragon's Teeth at the water's edge; above you in the trees, especially when the foliage is at its thinnest, you will see Fort Henry and behind it a gun position from the invasion scare days (note how its field of fire was completely blocked by the newer structure - a sign of Britain's growing confidence that the threat of invasion

was well past?). As you leave the beach, note the defused sea mine acting as a charity collecting box for the Shipwrecked Fishermen and Mariners Royal Benevolent Fund, with the poignant words inscribed on it - 'There is sorrow on the sea' - particularly meaningful if you consider the sorrow caused to the seamen of many nations who were lost or wounded off the Dorset coast as casualties to unforgiving and undiscriminating mines.

Not readily visible to all are the seven Valentine Duplex Drive tanks that lie below the waters of the Bay. These tanks, designed to 'swim' ashore on an assault beach, were lost during trials - trials, though, that ultimately led to the successful Sherman DD tanks. The wreck sites are regularly dived by local SCUBA enthusiasts.

A rather unusual circular pillbox (possibly a 'Type 26') can be found beyond the headland (only accessible from this direction at low tide), beyond which again some Project Fougasse pipes may be seen at low water; however, instead of walking on the rocks below Redend Point, particularly if the tide is in, the pillbox and oil pipe artifacts can be reached by taking the track to the beach by the Banks' Arms Hotel.

Near the geologically fascinating Agglestone on Studland Heath (at SZ 025833) you can see the remains of other defensive structures. Take the bridleway off the road to the Sandbanks Ferry just to the south of the Knoll House Hotel and continue along it until its junction with the footpath to the Agglestone: the two sunken pillboxes are located on knolls to the right-hand side of the track. Finally, note in the grounds opposite the Knoll House Hotel the remains of one of the Fougasse pumping stations.

A sea mine, now a charity collecting box on the footpath leading inland from Middle Beach.

TYNEHAM VALLEY LIGHT ANTI-AIRCRAFT GUN POSITION

OS: SY 893811

Location: On the right-hand side of the road leading down from Whiteway Hill to Tyneham.

Today the original use of the structure is still quite obvious.

I can find no record to identify positively this gun post; I believe it to be have been for a 20 mm light anti-aircraft gun of the US Army, probably manned by personnel of the 184th LAA Battalion. As can be seen, it commanded a good field of fire seawards towards Worbarrow Bay.

TYNEHAM VILLAGE   OS: SY 882802 (car park)

Location: Below Whiteway Hill, off the unclassified road between Stoborough/ Corfe Castle and East Lulworth.

The Purbeck village of Tyneham's first contribution to the war effort was the giving up of Tyneham House to the RAF for use as WAAF accommodation and as an officers' mess when an RAF unit - RAF Brandy Bay - was established on the top of nearby Gad Cliff (SY 885797) as the Monitor and Control Station for the Southern Gee Chain. The RAF moved out of the manor house in 1943 when, on the direct orders of the War Cabinet, the whole village and over 3,000 acres of the surrounding farmland around it were requisitioned for battle training purposes in the build-up to 'Overlord'; little did the inhabitants of this beautiful spot dream that they would not be able to return to their homes when hostilities were over. With their worldly possessions about them, the villagers pulled out with a sense of patriotism and national duty - leaving a poignant notice on the church door asking that it, and their houses, be treated with care. The area served its purpose well in training those who were to land on 'the far shore', but was never returned to private ownership - and for many years was barred completely to public access.

Today what remains of the village, except for the church and school, is but a set of 'restored ruins'. Exhibitions of Tyneham's social and natural history can be seen in both the school room and the church (which remains undamaged and as beautiful as ever). Sadly, rendered dangerous by live firing exercises, Tyneham House has been damaged beyond economic repair. In the main, light armoured fighting vehicles such as Scorpions use this part of the Lulworth Ranges for battle training - and access to Tyneham is normally restricted to weekends and the month of August; it is dangerous to deviate from the marked footpaths.

The heart of the old village today, with Post Office Row in the foreground and, beyond a Range Warden's Land Rover, the Parish Church of St Mary.

Now saved from further decay, but demonstrating so clearly how young men training for war brought them to the very edge of complete destruction, Taylor's Cottages still stand in Tyneham as a 'restored ruin' under the watchful eye of today's Army.

UPTON FORT

OS: SY 742815

Location: Alongside the Dorset Coast Path, half a mile east of the village of Osmington Mills. To reach the fort proceed via the Coast Path, from either Osmington Mills or Ringstead, or if approaching by road leave the A353 on the minor road to Osmington Mills and then, after half a mile, proceed on foot to the end of the first track on your left.

Designed to supplement the other gun batteries guarding Weymouth Bay and the approaches to Portland Harbour, the Upton Battery became operational in 1902 (as a wall plate still in situ 'ER 1902' indicates) and was to be equipped with two 6-inch and two 9.2-inch breech-loading guns mounted above sunken magazines; the former guns, however, were probably never provided. Support build-ings were positioned behind and to the west of the gun positions, but a plan to build a pier below the site for provisioning was never proceeded with. The site was placed on care and maintenance after the First World War and the guns removed.

With the outbreak of the second war, plans were made to bring Upton back to an operational status, and some time between June 1940 and January 1941 the battery was equipped with two 6-inch naval guns from the scrapped battleship HMS *Erin* (which previously served with the Turkish Navy as the *Reshadieh*). The guns were installed on the old 9.2-inch platforms, suitably modified to take the

Viewed from seaward is one of the two 9.2-inch gun positions (fitted with 6-inch guns during the Second World War). Note the gun mounting bolts still in situ, together with the railings behind them.

new weapons, and the original magazines were once again utilised for their design purpose. The main armament was augmented by a 4.5-inch howitzer of French origin and light anti-aircraft weapons, the battery being manned by troops of the 522nd (Dorset) Coastal Regiment.

The guns were only once fired in anger when, on the night of 21 March 1944, they opened fire against marauding German E-boats on the edge of Weymouth Bay.

All of the country's Coastal Defence Batteries were decommissioned by 1956 and Fort Upton is today in private ownership, with most of the ancillary buildings in use as either permanent or holiday homes - and enjoying the magnificent views that exist from here across Weymouth Bay to the Isle of Portland. The magazines and battery sites are still in good enough condition to show clearly their origin, and in addition to the main buildings secondary structures can be seen between the fort and the Coast Path.

Left **An accommodation block between the gun positions (utilised as a shelter, gasproof lobby and dressing station) with the two westernmost gun positions beyond.**

Below left **A defensive position, with the main structure just visible in the background.**

Below **An observation post, alongside which runs the Dorset Coast Path.**

VERNE CITADEL

OS: SY 691738 (North Gate)

> Location: Portland Heights, signposted 'HM Prison The Verne' from Fortuneswell, or by passing the RN memorial and continuing eastward along Priory Road past the Portland Heights Hotel.

The initial work on the construction of the 56-acre Verne Citadel commenced in 1848, the stone excavated from the dry moat being utilised in the construction of the breakwaters in Portland Harbour. The first sections were completed in 1861, with much of the labour being supplied by prisoners from the nearby prison (now a Young Offenders Institute); records indicate that the Citadel was completed in its amended design form by 1881. The muzzle-loading guns with which the Verne was equipped were rapidly becoming obsolete, and by 1906 the fort, having been redesignated as an infantry barracks three years earlier, was devoid of all heavy armament.

On the outbreak of war the Coastal Artillery headquarters was moved to the Verne from Weymouth's Red Barracks, and in 1941 a coastal defence radar set was set up at the Verne on one of the original gunpits, being operational until early in 1945. Until the nearby 3.7-inch AA battery became operational just to the west of the Citadel (see separate entry, page 71), a battery of First World War-vintage 3-inch AA guns were positioned on the glacis as a stop-gap air defence

The main (North) entrance to the Citadel. The outer steel barred gate is still in position, as is the suspended portcullis above. Note the iron-clad rifle 'loops'.

measure. During attacks on Portland by the Luftwaffe the Verne was bombed, but its inherent strength - and an element of good luck - meant that casualties were minimal.

In 1944, with the build-up to D-Day in full swing, stores and ammunition were again housed in some of the magazines, while the original main magazine was converted to a hospital and mortuary in anticipation of heavy casualties from Normandy, which, happily, were nowhere near as numerous as had been feared.

RAF The Verne

From September 1943, on a redundant gun positon within the walls of the Verne Citadel, there stood an RAF Chain Home 'extra low' radar station, tasked against low-flying aircraft and offshore shipping movements. The mast was over 200 feet high and radar returns could be obtained from as far away as the French coast. Personnel from RAF The Verne had the additional responsibility of servicing the Army's coastal radar station at nearby Eastcliff. The wartime equipment - Type 277 - was replaced in the post-war modernisation of the RAF radar system by a 'Rotor' station - which, apart from the transmitter head, was located underground in a built-up mound at the eastern end of the moat.

Ironically, what was built by largely convict labour is now a prison, for the Verne Citadel was transferred to the Home Office at the end of the 1940s and the present establishment opened in 1950. Naturally, the vast majority of the site is closed to the public, but worthwhile views can be obtained from the public highways at both entrances and from nearby public footpaths.

The former main magazine (*below*), converted as an emergency hospital and mortuary as part of the D-Day preparations (*left*).

WARDON HILL HOSPITAL OS: ST 610028

Location: On the A37 road from
Dorchester to Yeovil.

Replacing a sprawling British Army camp located here and extending eastward as far as the tumuli on East Hill (OS: ST 622025) and down almost to the village of Sydling St Nicholas, this United States military hospital, on land once owned by Winchester College, was specifically built for the receipt of casualties from the battlefields of Europe from D-Day onwards.

The 1944 Commanding Officer of this large hutted hospital, Colonel Otto, claimed that it was the best equipped in the whole of Southern England, having nine operating theatres, all of which worked without a break for the first two weeks of the Normandy campaign. Casualties tended were not exclusively American, for French soldiers and members of the Maquis were also treated at Wardon Hill, with wounded personnel being in theatre in little over 8 hours after leaving France.

In addition to the medical facilities provided, the hospital boasted its own cinema and theatre, together with the inevitable baseball pitch. And, of course, Wardon Hill produced its own fresh baked bread, doughnuts and ice-cream!

With the fighting over, the hospital closed down in 1945 and the buildings were then surrounded by security fencing and watch-towers and the site used as a

A general view of the site today, with hospital roads and hut bases still clearly visible.

prisoner-of-war camp until the last repatriations had taken place.

Today the area once occupied by the hospital has a variety of uses: the Clay Pigeon Shoot has been here since the 1950s, the Clay Pigeon Kart Club commenced operations in the 1960s and the Caravan Site was established during the following decade. There is also a busy transport cafe on the site (located where the ambulance garage once stood).

The remaining artifacts to be seen are the hospital water tower (less its storage tank) and mortuary building, the former having a clay pigeon (skeet) trap on its roof and the latter, now extensively rebuilt, being used for storage. Both are clearly visible from the public footpath running from the sharp bend in the unclassified road off the A37 immediately north of the kart track down towards the hamlet of Up Sydling. Around the racing circuit you can still see the remains of building foundations and roadways and, at the time of writing, the hospital drainage system is being restored for use by the current owners.

From the original British Army camp, on private land around ST 639007 (just north of Sydling St Nicholas), the remains of two rifle range butts and a single Nissen hut can still be seen.

Also of interest is the post-war Royal Observer Corps post, next to the futuristic-looking green dome which is an automatic weather reporting station, and the stand of new trees on the other side of the A37, planted in 1992 to commemorate the local Home Guard unit who had a base here.

The hospital water tower base. The bore hole below was not a success, so water was pumped here from nearby Up Sydling - sometimes at the rate of over 45,000 US gallons a day.

WEST MOORS PETROL DEPOT

OS: SU 078037

> Location: On the B3072, between West Moors village and Verwood.

Originally planned as an ammunition depot, the 430-acre installation at West Moors has, in fact, always been used for the bulk storage and distribution of fuels and lubricants. Construction work started on the site in 1939, for use by British forces, but by August 1943 the American 3877th Quartermaster Gas (ie petrol) Supply Company was in residence, the base being designated as POL (Petrol, Oil and Lubricants) Depot Q-328 with the allotted task of the storage of petrol scheduled for shipment to France. At its peak the depot stored about 75,000 tons of petrol in 5-gallon jerricans, and lesser amounts of diesel fuel, plus a wide range of oils and lubricants (the vast majority of which was manhandled). Despite being such an obvious and attractive target, West Moors received remarkably little attention from the Luftwaffe - this could, in some part, be due to the effectiveness of the dummy camouflaged site set up in the nearby Verwood sandpits to look like a petrol depot! A close miss adjacent to the Station Headquarters building was the nearest the depot came to receiving any meaningful damage.

Depot Q-328 reverted to British control in July 1945 and from 1946 the Royal Army Service Corps was in residence as No 9 Petroleum Depot, control passing to the Ordnance Corps in 1965 following an Army reorganisation. The title of Petroleum Centre dates from 1971, while the current title of Petroleum Centre, Royal Logistics Corps dates from the formation of the RLC on 5 April 1993.

Today the depot is the Army's only such establishment. It is responsible for the resupply of petroleum products to the Army in both peace and war, and a host of support, training and research functions. Ongoing modernisation has resulted in little being recognisable from the war years, except for a very short section of the internal railway line and the site at the Fairfax complex (of US Army vintage) where aspects of technical training now take place but which, unfortunately, is not visible to the public. Nevertheless, from the road that passes alongside, one can appreciate the size (the perimeter fence runs for 5 miles) and importance of this, one of Dorset's few active military bases 50 years after the end of the Second World War.

The camp entrance off the B3072, with storage tanks visible on the left.

WEST STAFFORD HOME GUARD HUT

OS: SY 745896

Location: 1 mile east of West Stafford at the junction of the roads to Crossways and Woodsford.

Used as the headquarters of the local Home Guard Unit, with a commitment to the defence of RAF Warmwell and the manning of some of the Frome Valley pillboxes among its roles, the hut stands today as a silent reminder of the efforts of local volunteer soldiers, most of whom were too old or young for regular military service, or were in reserved occupations.

Its duties completed, the Home Guard was stood down on 3 December 1944. Today the hut is in a state of disrepair, but still finds some limited use as a farm building.

The West Stafford Home Guard hut.

WEST WEARS (BLACKNOR FORT) COASTAL DEFENCE BATTERY

OS: SY 679716

Location: On the west side of Portland, approximately half way between the Bill and Priory Corner, approached via the coastal footpath or by the public footpath alongside Portland Cemetery in Weston Road.

Completed in 1901, the West Wears Battery, or Blacknor Fort as it is sometimes known locally, occupied a commanding position above Lyme Bay and the western approach to the strategic Island of Portland, and was also in an excellent position to provide enfilading fire along Chesil Beach in the event of amphibious troops attempting a landing there. The Second World War heavy gun fit was of two 9.2-inch Mk X breech-loading weapons with a range of some 16 miles, while light anti-aircraft weapons were provided for point defence, one of which was credited with shooting down a Dornier Do 17, which fell on Chesil Beach.

Rumours that the 9.2-inch guns were fired for the only time in anger on the night of 27/28 April 1944 during the ill-fated Exercise 'Tiger', when German E-boats ran amok amongst US amphibious forces rehearsing for the D-Day landings, appear to be unfounded. I am advised, although only second-hand, that the radar plot was too confused to tell friend from foe and that the guns did not open up for fear of hitting the American landing ships instead of the enemy vessels.

Today the property is in private owner-ship - cottages and a riding stables - but the origins of the buildings are still quite obvious and much of a military nature still stands in reasonably good repair and in everyday use. Note, in addition to the main structure, the searchlight base alongside the coastal path below the fort.

The central area of the site today; the gun platforms are to seaward of these buildings.

WEYMOUTH 40 mm BOFORS LIGHT ANTI-AIRCRAFT GUN POSITION

OS: SY 67388

Location: Off Newstead Road, Weymouth, to the rear of the Asda Supermarket, on the old Weymouth to Portland railway line.

This gun position was sited to give low-level AA defence to the Weymouth Harbour area, being a purpose-built stone structure set into a railway embankment.

Today the site is in good condition and, being of stone instead of the more usual concrete, has withstood the ravages of time. The firing platform still possesses the gun mounting ring, and of the rooms below, reached by a set of steps on the southern side of the position, only the doors are missing.

Note the gun-mounting plinth, together with the dividing partitions from the ready-use ammunition lockers and general equipment storage cupboards.

ROYAL AIR FORCE

BALLARD DOWN RANGE

OS: SZ 044814 (Radar Unit)

> Location: A cliff-top plateau lying between Studland village and the town of Swanage.

The peaceful views today from Ballard Down towards the Isle of Wight, Poole Harbour and Swanage Bay bear little resemblance to the hectic activity that took place here during 1943 and 1944. In those years this area of downland was used as an air-to-ground range by the pilots of fighter-bomber aircraft sharpening their skills for the battle to free Europe - and epitomised by the carnage wrought amongst retreating German armour in the killing ground of the Falaise Gap in August 1944. Typhoons roared overhead as they fired unguided rockets, or opened up with cannon, using the old tanks and vehicles positioned here as targets. (Ironically, it is almost certain that some of these same armoured fighting vehicles would, earlier in the war when the flow of battle was running the other way, have been used as 'stop-gap' strong points.)

The range was controlled from a hardened Range Control Post responsible for range safety and flying control, the remains of which can still be found adjacent to the trig point above Ballard Cliff, approached on the Dorset Coast Path from either the Studland or Swanage directions. (The adjacent earth banks are the remains of a Victorian rifle range.)

The remains of the RAF Range Control Post on Ballard Down.

BROWNSEA ISLAND DECOY SITE

OS: SZ 012881

> Location: The western end of Brownsea Island, between the remains of Maryland village and the present firebreak.

In 1941 a Major Night Strategic Decoy Site - known as a Starfish Site and manned here by RAF personnel - was established on the uninhabited end of Brownsea island to decoy bomber aircraft away from the important towns of Poole and Bournemouth, and is considered by local residents to have well proved its worth, for on one night alone 190 bombs are reputed to have dropped on Brownsea Island instead of their intended targets!

The site was controlled from a concrete bunker about 200 yards away from the Decoy Site, and consisted of tanks of inflammable liquids into which bath-tubs of water were irregularly flushed to give off clouds of steam and thus the impression of bursting bombs. The former pottery workers' village of Maryland was extensively damaged during the decoyed raids and was razed to the ground by the Royal Marines in 1963.

Today the control bunker is invisible beneath heavy growth; however, a prominent air raid shelter and an ancillary building (possibly an ammunition store) can be seen from the National Trust pathway at SZ 016877 and SZ 016881 respectively.

The air raid shelter adjacent to the Decoy Site.

RAF BULBARROW HILL

OS: ST 781057
(Domestic Site)

Location: Bulbarrow Hill, 7 miles west of Blandford Forum, approachable on minor roads from four different directions.

RAF Bulbarrow Hill, which became operational in 1942, was the Master Station for the Southern Gee Chain, its Slave Stations being at Thruleigh Hill in Sussex and West Prawle, Devon. (Gee was a medium range navigation system, with which an aircraft or ship within reception range was able to plot accurately its position at the interception of the hyperbolic range circles transmitted by the Gee stations.)

The RAF unit, by then reduced to one officer and 28 airmen, closed down on 1 December 1957, but the United States Air Force later maintained a communications facility at Bulbarrow Hill, which worked in close liaison with the USAF Troposcatter Relay Station at the old Ringstead Chain Home radar station.

Today a small part of the site is still in military ownership, with MOD communication masts standing adjacent to where the 240-foot-high wooden wartime transmitter towers once stood, the bases of one of which are still visible next to the postwar power room in the field east of the modern structures and opposite the

The domestic site today, where enough wartime buildings remain standing for the modern visitor to feel the presence still of those who served here in years long ago.

entrance to the domestic site. (The second mast was located where the isolated clump of trees stands.)

The former administration and accommodation site is now occupied by Bulbarrow Timber Products. Over a dozen Nissen (and similar) huts still remain in various states of disrepair, together with a single air raid shelter and two water towers. The camp's self-contained water and sewage system also remains in situ.

The sites, both modern and wartime, are not open to the public; however, almost all the artifacts are visible from the roadside, and the views from this hilltop beauty spot are second to none in the county!

Left Yesterday and today: the modern Ministry of Defence communications tower, with a wartime hardened building in the foreground.

Below The concrete bases of one of the wartime towers, to the right of the post-war building.

RAF CHICKERELL

OS: SY 655796

Location: Off Radipole Lane, on the northern outskirts of Weymouth.

The military airfield at Chickerell was one of the many established around the coast of the British Isles in 1918 for use by land-based aircraft in the anti-submarine role, but its use was short-lived, as was its subsequent use as a civil aerodrome.

For some obscure reason, RAF Chickerell is not listed as an active RAF unit during the Second World War - but it certainly was! The airstrip's main role was in support of activities on the Chesil Beach Bombing Ranges, it saw occasional use as an emergency landing ground (although its short grass runways limited the size of aircraft able to operate from here), and even saw limited use during the Battle of Britain as a dispersal and alert site for fighter aircraft deployed from RAF Warmwell. When an Air Sea Rescue unit was established at Weymouth Harbour in April 1944, its personnel were billeted at Chickerell, and remained there until the ASR unit's disbandment in 1946.

In the post-war years the Army Air Corps and the Fleet Air Arm both made use of the Chickerell airstrip, USAF personnel from the Tropospheric Scatter Base at Ringstead were accommodated in the wartime RAF huts, and the local Air Cadet Squadron was based there - all to come to an end when the military gave up ownership in 1959.

Today there is precious little evidence of the former use of this corner of Weymouth, almost all of the airfield having been built on for residential and industrial purposes. The old entrance to the site remains as a small patch of concrete opposite 459 Radipole Lane (and almost opposite Westhaven County Junior School), and adjacent Cobham Drive maintains a link, in name only, with Chickerell's short association with civilian flying.

Today's only link with history - the old camp entrance.

RAF CHRISTCHURCH

OS: SZ 186932

Location: On the east of the town of the same name, lying alongside the A337 road to Lymington.

Opened as a flying club site in 1935 and closed in the same month that war broke out, having always experienced financial problems, the site was requisitioned in the spring of 1940 as the main support airfield for the newly established Telecommunications Research Establishment at Worth Matravers. This unit was joined later in the year by an Anti-Aircraft Co-operation Unit flying Fairey Battles and, at the same time, a 'shadow' aircraft factory was commissioned, which was run by Airspeed Ltd and used for the production of that company's Oxford multi-crew trainer. By

August of 1941, with the TRE support aircraft withdrawn and the AACU flight disbanded, Christchurch was designated as a satellite airfield for RAF Hurn - and Airspeed's activities continued to expand. Horsa gliders were amongst the aircraft now being produced at Christchurch.

In the build-up to 'Overlord', and with the previously short runway extended and laid with a 4,800-foot wire-mesh overlay, units of the USAAF moved here to fly intruder operations over mainland Europe. Even in its extended state, the runway was short for the resident heavily laden fighter-bombers, and a number of crashes occurred, including one of a Thunderbolt in April 1944 that led to 19 deaths.

Former aircraft factory buildings; the new road in the foreground is aptly named 'The Runway'.

With the end of the war looming on the horizon, Airspeed made Christchurch its main South Coast base and, apart from its activities, a mantle of relative peace fell upon the airfield, which was eventually transferred to the Ministry of Aircraft Production in 1946. A hard runway was laid and aircraft such as the Ambassador airliner and Vampire, Venom and, later, Sea Vixen jets all flew from here - as did gliders of No 622 (Air Cadet) Gliding School, and the local aero club. Aircraft production ceased in 1962, and the airfield closed in 1967.

Today Siemens are installed at the former aircraft factory site, where the wartime buildings still rub shoulders with many of a more modern design. In a pair of small factory units in Airfield Way, Beagle Aircraft Ltd maintains the site's link with aviation, being involved in the manufacture of lightweight components for aircraft simulators.

Of the airfield itself there is now no trace, housing and industrial development having spread rapidly over its grass expanse. Even its old boundaries are hard to define, but they were loosely Mudeford Lane (west), Highcliffe Road (east), Bure Lane (south) and Grange Road (north); the new road called The Runway is not really aligned with the old flight strip, but does give a general indication of where the centre of the airfield once lay. Nevertheless, the past history of the area is well highlighted by the names of the modern streets: Lysander Close, Blenheim Drive, Dakota Close, Halifax Way and Airspeed Road to name but a few associated with the war years.

Finally, as a tribute to Christchurch's association with the aircraft-manufacturing industry, a well-preserved Sea Vixen stands on a plinth alongside Somerford Road (near the A35/A337 roundabout).

A current link with aviation: the Beagle Aircraft industrial unit, which makes lightweight bodies for flight simulators. (An MD-90 airliner simulator cockpit is visible inside, plus a children's activity mock-up of an F-18 Hornet fighter.)

RAF HAMWORTHY

OS: SZ 036896
and (Technical Site) SY 986903

Location: The northern shores of
Poole Harbour, the Operations Area being
at Salternes Marina, near Lilliput on the
B3369 Poole to Sandbanks Road,
and the Technical Site being near the
Dorset Yacht Company Yard at
Lake Drive, Lake.

With the anti-U-boat war not running in
the Allies' favour in 1942, RAF Coastal
Command sought a site for a flying boat
base to supplement those at Mount Batten
and Pembroke Dock; Poole Harbour was
chosen and RAF Poole, which was
renamed RAF Hamworthy prior to receiving its first aircraft (Sunderlands of 461
Sqn of the Royal Australian Air Force)
became operational in August of that year.

The base lacked dedicated support or
domestic facilities, workshops, offices or
billets, and a large number of local houses
were taken over to rectify this major short-
coming. A slipway for maintenance was,
however, constructed - but even that was
far smaller than desirable.

The premises of the Poole Harbour
Yacht Club, in Sandbanks Road, were
taken over as the Operational HQ and the
Harbour Heights Hotel, in Haven Road,
was commandeered as the Officers' Mess.
In April 1943 the Sunderlands were
replaced by Catalinas of 210 Sqn, which
continued to operate their long-range

**68 Lake Drive - once (before the sloped roof
was fitted) the control room/watch office for
flying activities in Poole Harbour.**

patrols from here until the base closed to military operations around Christmastime 1943 when the needs of the Combined Operations Base HMS *Turtle* became paramount. The Technical Site saw no further aviation activity, but the Salternes area was handed over to the Civil Aviation Authority for use as a passenger terminal for BOAC flying boat passengers. BOAC's activities ceased here at the end of March 1948, when its operations transferred to Southampton.

Today one could be excused for passing through here without being aware of the use of Poole Harbour by military flying boats (although the story of the BOAC aircraft is well known). Two ex-military 'Maycrete' huts still stand just inside the entrance to Salternes Marina and the Harbour Heights Hotel and the Poole Harbour Yacht Club premises still command breathtaking views across the harbour to the Purbecks. The latter building,

now the Salternes Hotel, contains the area where the operations room and the CO's office were located.

Looking back towards the town from the Marina's boat yard you are viewing the main area where the flying boats were moored between sorties. The Royal Marines Landing Craft Base occupies the former Technical Site; however, the slipway that is visible from the road outside formerly belonged to the Dorset Yacht Company and is not the one used to haul Sunderlands or Catalinas out of the water for repairs - that has now been built over.

Today, sadly, there is no plaque anywhere to record the bravery of those who operated from RAF Hamworthy.

The rear of the Salternes Hotel and Poole Harbour Yacht Club premises today. The Base Operations Rooms was located in the room to the left of the modern glass-covered veranda.

RAF HURN

OS: SZ 115980

> Location: Bournemouth International Airport (well signposted).

The RAF airfield at Hurn, to the north of Bournemouth and Christchurch and bounded by the Rivers Stour and Moors, was opened in the summer of 1941 as a satellite for RAF Ibsley, which lay just over the border in Hampshire. Some of the first productive flights were in support of TRE at Worth Matravers, but its first major role was as a base for the Whitley aircraft of No 297 and 296 Squadrons, which came here in the summer of 1942 and operated in the paratroop training role; they also had the secondary role of dropping propaganda leaflets over occupied France.

In March of 1944 the three resident RAF squadrons (295, 296 and 570, flying Albemarle aircraft) were replaced by a Wing of the Royal Canadian Air Force, flying deadly Typhoon fighter-bombers, which were soon in operation over Northern France. Other new arrivals included a force of Mosquito night fighters for protection against the anticipated Luftwaffe reprisal air raids (which only rarely materialised). The final offensive sorties flown from Hurn were by B-26 Marauders of the USAAF, mainly against rail centres; then, in October 1944, the airfield was handed over to BOAC when the world of civil aviation began to open up again as German international strength rapidly faded away.

The wartime guardroom serves a similar purpose today; it is now the building used by the Airport Security Organisation.

In the final months of the European War and the immediate post-war period Hurn, now in the hands of the Ministry of Civil Aviation, was extremely busy as the country's major international airport - and continued so until Heathrow opened as London Airport at the beginning of 1946. In the years since then Hurn has not found it easy to make financial ends meet for, despite its best efforts and runway improvements to permit higher take-off weights by civilian airliners, traffic figures have never achieved their hoped-for levels. It has sometimes been at its busiest when Heathrow and/or Gatwick are fog-bound and arriving aircraft are diverted here to the sanctuary of Bournemouth's well-equipped (twin ILS/DME) runway.

Today Hurn bears the title Bournemouth International Airport and serves as a busy regional airport (with 90,000 movements in 1994) serving central southern England, and has a number of schedule, charter and cargo operators based there. Additionally, to the north of the main runway is the base of FR Aviation, which carries out contract flying for the Ministry of Defence as well as aircraft maintenance work. The Civil Aviation Authority's College of Air Traffic Control is also based at the aerodrome and there is still a small RAF presence in the form of the Chipmunk T10 aircraft of No 2 Air Experience Flight, used to provide flying opportunities for Air Cadets.

Although, like the very modern-styled passenger terminal building, there are many new structures at Hurn, it is surprising just how many buildings if 1940s vintage remain - not just Second World War hangars, but a miscellany of smaller buildings as well - all providing a very positive link with this important airfield's interesting historical past.

No longer the major operational airfield that it was during the Second World War, the military presence today, apart from visiting aircraft, is confined to Chipmunk aircraft of No 2 Air Experience Flight, RAF. Note the Hunter and Sea Hawk of Jet Heritage, and a 1940s 'Maycrete' hut in the left background.

RAF LYME REGIS

OS: SY 335915

> Location: The Cobb, and to its immediate
> west, Lyme Regis - all easily visible from
> the public highway.

Having been established in 1937 to provide support facilities for aircraft using the ranges off Chesil Beach, the base was ideally situated to provide Air Sea Rescue services when war broke out, although the initially allocated craft lacked seaworthiness and were supplemented by a Belgian rescue craft, *Ministre Lippens*. Initially not as busy as some of the ASR bases further east along the Channel coast, No 37 Air Sea Rescue Marine Craft Unit (as it was officially titled from 1942) nevertheless played an important part in ensuring that the ASR motto 'The Sea Shall Not Have Them' was upheld, with 65 lives being saved by the unit during the war years.

The unit remained in existence until July 1964, parented by RAF Exeter after the post-war closure of RAF Warmwell, with its ASR commitment gradually lessening as helicopters took over more and more of this vital task (and by which time the term Air Sea Rescue - ASR - had been replaced by Search & Rescue - SAR).

Today the headquarters building is an adventure training centre (with a commemorative plaque on its wall), the RAF boat yard is a car park and the unit slipway can be clearly seen next to that of the RNLI - who continue the rescue tradition of Lyme Regis with a modern Atlantic 21 inshore rescue boat.

The RAF slipway, used to recover and launch ASR and range vessels for maintenance. It was not used to launch vessels 'lifeboat style'!

The HQ and Administrative building today. Note the lookout room at the near end of the building and the commemorative plaque to the right of the right-hand door.

OBSERVER CORPS POST, DORCHESTER

OS: SY 683911

Location: Within Poundbury Rings, Poundbury Road, Dorchester (access via a stile opposite the end of Normandy Way).

Although it is often said that the British Chain High and Chain Low radar stations were the greatest scientific aid to this country in its victory in the Battle of Britain and in the years of Luftwaffe attacks on the country that followed, it is equally often forgotten that the technology available in those days was such that radar tracking of aircraft was virtually impossible once the raiders had made a landfall, the target echoes being lost in 'ground returns'. To combat this a chain of lookout posts, manned by members of the Observer Corps (later Royal Observer Corps), was established to make visual contact with and report on enemy aircraft overflying the British Isles. One of the many Dorset posts - an average of 20 at any one time during the war years - was that established at Poundbury Rings, Dorchester.

In the post-war years the ROC's tasking changed and its main role was one of reporting and monitoring nuclear fall-out in the event of an attack on the UK. Enthusiasm for aircraft recognition, nevertheless, remained as widespread as ever, with members of the Corps still being acknowledged as 'The Experts' in this specialist field. With the ending of the Cold War, the Royal Observer Corps was stood down in 1991.

The above-ground element of the post-war ROC monitoring post within the ancient monument of Poundbury Rings. The wartime 'sand and railway sleeper' lookout stood on the rings to the rear.

RAF RINGSTEAD

OS: SY 748819 (Operational Site Entrance);
SY 742831 (Domestic Site)

Location: The Operations Site was to the west of the coastal village of Ringstead, and the Domestic Site at Upton, just south of the A353 road.

RAF Ringstead was one of the westward additions to the radar chain along the South Coast of England, and entered service after the Battle of Britain had been won, but well before the Allies were assured of final victory. Work on the station commenced in January 1941 and the unit became operational in May of the following year with both Chain Home (CH) and Chain Home Low (CHL) transmitter/receivers. As well as its primary aircraft surveillance role, RAF Ringstead had a secondary role of shipping surveillance.

Initially, the operational buildings were above ground and unhardened. Attempts to find a suitable site for a reserve station at either Bowleaze Cove (circa SY 703820) or Osmington Mills (circa SY 735817) were unsuccessful due to problems with either large local buildings or topography, so in later years the main operational buildings were protected by earthworks alongside and over the top.

The unit continued in service after the end of the war and was still operating in 1956 as one of the post-war 'Rotor Radar Stations'. From December 1963 No 6 Detachment of the USAF 2180 Communications Squadron operated a Tropospheric Scatter System link at Ringstead, this being closed in 1974 and the two massive aerial arrays being demolished by March of the following year.

Today there is still much to be seen of interest. At Upton, just after leaving the A353 main road (signposted Ringstead) near Poxwell, you will find the unit's Motor Transport Garage on your right-hand side and shortly after, on your left,

The sealed-off entrance to the westernmost bunker, which once housed one of the radar receivers.

you will see the base of the former guard-room and the steps leading up to it. Here can also be seen, together with miscellaneous building foundations, the Sergeants' Mess, one of the WAAF accommodation huts (both behind the guardroom) and a former stores building (opposite).

Continuing towards the coast, you will pass through a steep-sided valley (from which Group Captain Jim Stagg, Eisenhower's Chief Meteorologist, watched shipping leave Portland Harbour on D-Day) and a pillbox on the right. Next, take the footpath off to the right of the tarmac road, and behind the first bungalow on the left can be seen one of the covered operational buildings. Follow the footpath to the right and turn left at the marker 'Coast Path ½', shortly after which a second covered bunker will be seen in the trees.

Continue straight ahead where the main path goes to the right (and into the former USAF aerial site) and you will shortly find the concrete bases of one of the CH aerials - the size of which will give some appreciation of how massive the wooden aerial structures were. The other CH aerial base (rather more overgrown) is reached by turning right along the coastal footpath, ahead over a small bridge, and right again at the next footpath. Fort Upton (see separate entry, page 83) is on your left as you move inland and find the final protected bunker in the trees on the right - the only one of the three where any of the former structure is clearly visible. To return to the entrance to the operational area, turn right at the footpath junction ahead of you.

The former Sergeants' Mess building still standing at Upton.

RAF TARRANT RUSHTON OS: ST 946058

Location: 3 miles east of Blandford Forum, north of the B3082 Wimborne Minster to Blandford Forum road.

Built on a plateau above the Tarrant Valley, with the hill fortress of Badbury Rings as a backdrop, and completed in May 1943 as an Airborne Forces airfield, RAF Tarrant Rushton was the main base from which the 6th Airborne Division departed for the first landings against the German forces defending Northern France in the earliest hours of D-Day. The *coup de main* against the bridges over the Caen Canal and the River Orne was executed by troops of the Oxford & Buckinghamshire Light Infantry who had flown out of 'TR'. In the year or so prior to this, Tarrant Rushton had been almost exclusively involved in the training and build-up of these forces, the main exception being SOE-sponsored air-drop missions flown in support of the French Resistance.

With 'Overlord' successfully accomplished, some smaller airborne operations were flown, with the tug aircraft reverting to their pure bomber role when not thus engaged; additionally, Tarrant Rushton acted as a reception airhead for seriously wounded casualties from the Normandy Campaign and later fighting in Europe, flown in for treatment at the local military hospitals.

A general view across Tarrant Rushton airfield, towards prehistoric Badbury Rings, from the northern threshold of the former main runway (01/19) - now just a farm track. In the distance can be seen the two remaining T2 hangars (left) and an aircraft shed. Note also the runway light fitting in the left foreground.

The last major airborne forces operation flown from here was that involved in the gallant, but unsuccessful, Operation 'Market Garden' - the assault on the Rhine bridges at Arnhem. The airfield operated, until the war ended, in the transport role and was placed on care and maintenance at the end of 1947. Flight Refuelling Ltd moved here in 1948 and almost immediately became involved in the Berlin Airlift.

In 1952 No 210 Advanced Flying School was formed at Tarrant Rushton, equipped with Meteor jets - with Flight Refuelling servicing and supporting the aircraft operations and the Royal Air Force providing the flying instructors. The airfield was also upgraded to act as a designated V-Force dispersal.

The end for this historical airfield came in September 1980, when Flight Refuelling Ltd closed down its operations and moved to Bournemouth International Airport (Hurn) from where, today, it continues its extensive and diverse aeronautical activities.

Today the airfield has been reclaimed for agricultural purposes, the three runways have been dug up (except for a strip of the north/south runway - 01/19 - which, together with the perimeter taxiway, are in use as farm tracks), and only two T2 hangars and an aircraft shed remain, together with a couple of Nissen huts. Additionally, on the cul-de-sac running northwards from almost opposite the old camp entrance, two of the ex-RAF buildings from the Communal Areas can still be seen, now in agricultural use.

The majority of service buildings outside the airfield's main boundary were located out to the north-east of the camp entrance - as was this structure, the only remaining building on the former No 3 Site.

THREE LEGGED CROSS AIRFIELD DECOY SITE

OS: SU 099069

> Location: On the northern edge of the golf course at Moor Valley Leisure Park. Turn off the B3072 into Potterne Way; from the car park proceed along the gravel path across the sports field, which turns towards the south-east, until you reach the edge of the golf course.

This was one of two Decoy Sites established to draw enemy aircraft away from the attractive target of the airfield at RAF Ibsley, a busy front-line operational airfield just across the county border in Hampshire. It was officially designated as a 'Q Site', and it consisted of a control bunker and generator room - strongly built and earth-covered - and a parallel strip of lights laid out in the form of runway lighting, supplemented by dummy aerodrome approach lights. Unlike some decoy sites, where mock aircraft were parked to simulate an aerodrome, this Q site was limited to night operations. It was manned by a small team of RAF personnel who were billeted in nearby Verwood.

Today the site is remarkably well preserved; the bunker is rust-free and the solid generator base is still in situ, as are the two blast walls at the entrance doors. The wiring itself was salvaged shortly after the end of the war.

The control bunker, with a golf course bunker in the foreground!

RAF TILLY WHIM

OS: SZ 032774

Location: Durlston Country Park, to the south of Swanage (well signposted).

The long-range navigation aid code-named 'Oboe', which was loosely based upon the German 'Lorenz' beam navigation system, was one of the war-winning electronic aids invented by the personnel of the Telecommunications Research Establishment (see Worth Matravers entry, page 115) to improve dramatically the bombing accuracy of the offensive aircraft of the RAF. It entered service in December 1942, being used operationally for the first time by Mosquito aircraft of 105 Sqn of Bomber Command's Pathfinder Force to target-mark during a precision attack on the power station at Lutterade in Holland.

In operation, radar frequency signals were directed towards the target area by a pair of co-operating ground stations in the UK, then re-transmitted back by the attacking aircraft by the use of a transpon-der. The bomber flew in a constant radius arc from the 'cat' station until intercepting the narrow bean from the 'mouse' station, the point where the two beams crossed being the exact position for the aircraft to drop its bombs (or release target-markers or illuminating flares).

RAF Tilly Whim, which normally operated in conjunction with the 'Oboe' stations at Beachy Head or Hawkshill Down, was equipped with a Type 9000 installation, and became operational in March 1944, fully supporting bomber operations (it was, for example, active for all of D-day) until the war moved out of range to the east. It was reduced to a care and maintenance status on 5 February 1945, and today the site is occupied by Durlston Country Park Information Centre, with a pictorial display regarding its RAF days on one of the walls.

No longer an 'Oboe' base, the transmitter site of RAF Tilly Whim is now the location of an Information Centre.

RAF WARMWELL

OS: SY 760885

Location: On the B3390, immediately to the west of the village of Crossways and 3½ miles south-east of Dorchester.

Opened in May 1937 as RAF Woodsford, an Armament Practice Camp to support the ranges off the Chesil Beach, it was renamed RAF Warmwell the following summer to avoid confusion with the Avro factory airfield at Woodford, Manchester. This airfield was a classic example of 'right place, right time', for it was ideally situated as a fighter base at the time of the Battle of Britain. Initially, Warmwell acted as a forward operating base for Spitfires of 609 Sqn from Middle Wallop - the aircraft flying in and out each day - but 152 Sqn's Spitfires were later permanently based at Warmwell, and together

these fighter aircraft enjoyed success against the German bombers attacking the Portland naval base and other South Coast targets.

The success was not, however, in one direction alone, and Warmwell itself came under heavy air attack on more than one occasion, with information released post-war revealing that one of the very first Ultra intercepts decoded was in connection with a planned attack on Warmwell. The heaviest damage, in terms of lives lost, was on 1 April 1941 when seven personnel were killed and another 18 injured. The aerodrome had a decoy site located

This building saw a variety of uses, including NAAFI, cinema and gymnasium. Today it continues to serve the local community well as a busy village hall. On its walls are displayed photographs of RAF Warmwell in its heyday, together with other memorabilia.

in nearby Knighton Woods, which sometimes succeeded in drawing fire away from the base. On the night of 14/15 May 1944, for example, the site was attacked three times instead of the camp itself.

As the war progressed and the Allies were able to go over to the offensive, fighter-bomber aircraft from Warmwell (Whirlwinds, Typhoons and, initially, Hurricanes) flew intruder sorties into Northern Europe. The base was also considered safe enough for armament practice camps, which had been suspended when the war was going so badly in 1940, to be resumed.

Although the Air Sea Rescue aircraft of 276 Sqn RAF (Walruses, Spitfires and Defiants) continued to be based there, in early 1944 the airfield became Station 454 of the USAAF and P-38 Lightnings arrived to carry out operations prior to, and in support of, the D-Day landings in Normandy. By August the USAAF had moved out to operate from sites nearer to the battle zones of France and the base returned to RAF control, until closure in 1946.

Today the vast majority of the runway areas have disappeared as gravel extraction has laid the area bare. Both wartime Bellman hangars remain, the control tower, with two 'panhandle' dispersals next to it, can still be seen as Egdon House at SY 762887 on the Crossways to West Stafford Road, and artifacts such as revetments and dispersal buildings can still be found in West Knighton Woods on the west of the site and, to a lesser extent, to the south of the B3390 (access via public footpaths). The gun harmonising butts can be see next to Oaklands Park, the Crossways village hall is a well-preserved ex-RAF building and the garden of a local bungalow boasts the (still almost complete) main anti-aircraft ammunition store! In Mount Skippet Way there is the attractive RAF Warmwell Memorial Stone, which is clearly signposted (see page 150).

Note: The Spitfire Mk 1A aircraft suspended on display at the Imperial War Museum in London is R6915, which served at RAF Warmwell with No 609 (West Riding) Squadron.

The former control tower, now a private house.

WORTH MATRAVERS

OS: SY 967777
(remaining TRE building)

Location: Land alongside the road and bridlepath running from Worth Matravers village to St Aldhelm's Head.

The Telecommunications Research Establishment on the windswept headland of St Aldhelm's (or St Alban's) was, without any doubt, one of the country's single most important defence research establishments during the whole of the Second World War, responsible for the vast majority of radar and radar-related research and development carried out at that time by British scientists in their quest to win the electronics war against the Axis Powers.

TRE moved south from Dundee to land around Renscombe Farm, on the outskirts of Worth Matravers, during the spring of 1940 and immediately continued its current research programme, setting out on new paths of research, on war-winning projects such as airborne radars (air-to-air intercept radars and air-to-surface anti-shipping/submarine and navigation radars), foil chaff, ground-based navigation systems and the analysis of German target identification systems such as 'Knickebeine'. TRE also devolved counter-electronics tactics to confuse bomber crews trying to use the beam system, and was also active in researching improvements to the country's air defence radar systems; in fact, the Chain Home and Chain Home Low systems at the site had the important secondary role of feeding information into the Fighter Command Operations Centre filter rooms.

The site was, therefore, quite correctly considered to be one of major strategic importance and, even allowing for the shortages of trained manpower and equipment available in the early days of the war, had a very respectable guard of some 135 troops, three 40 mm Bofors guns and a complement of light machine guns usable in the anti-aircraft or surface engagement roles. Amongst those serving at TRE were Dr D. W. Fry (to become the Director of Dorset's Atomic Energy Experimental Establishment at Winfrith) and Professor (later Sir) Bernard Lovell (who was to find fame at Jodrell Bank in later years).

In addition to the main establishment, research facilities were also set up in nearby Langton Matravers at the requisitioned Durnford School and Leeson House.

An event that took place across the English Channel on 28 February 1942 led directly to the main research activities at

The last remaining TRE building, this one on the former 'E' site. The stone in the foreground indicates where the base of one of the massive aerials once stood.

Worth and the surrounding area closing down: the commando raid on the German Wurzburg radar site at Bruneval, near Le Havre, during which the secret enemy equipment, which was the raid's target, was captured successfully - as was one of the operators. The captured equipment was analysed at Durnford House. It was felt that a 'retaliatory' raid on exposed Worth Matravers might be ordered by the Germans and Churchill gave his personal order that TRE was to move out 'before the next full moon' - which it duly did (but not quite within the Prime Minister's ordered time-scale), becoming re-established at Malvern, Worcestershire, by May 1942.

Rumours abound about a German raid on Worth Matravers, with a U-21 Volvo Penta outboard motor of the type used by German Commandoes having been recovered from the nearby seabed, but none have been substantiated.

This was not the end of all activities, however, and operational Gee and LORAN navigation systems continued to radiate from here, as - for a while - did the radar transmitters. The RAF moved out from Worth Matravers in 1958, although an 11-strong civilian party continued to be based here, operating the Gee transmitter site, until August 1963. The last of the aerial towers was demolished in November 1960.

RAF airstrip

A short airstrip was in use at Worth Matravers from early in 1940 until mid-1941, both for communications aircraft visiting TRE and as a landing site for gliders released off the Dorset coast and flying back towards the radar towers in the course of radar trials. It was located on the western side of the road leading from Renscombe Farm towards the cliff edge (OS: SY 963770), now just a large field! The main aircraft support for TRE was based at RAF Christchurch.

RAF Renscombe Down was a unit contained within the confines of RAF Worth Matravers - a training establishment involved, mainly, in preparing personnel for service with mobile radar and navigation aid detachments.

Today remarkably little can be seen of this once large establishment, although, of course, Durnford House and Leeson House are still standing at Langton Matravers. The only major building remaining is one on the former 'E' site, which is now in use as the Poole & Dorset Adventure Centre and has a few other building bases still in evidence around it, plus the site of an emergency water supply tank. There are odd patches of tarmac and concrete still to be seen, but precious little else.

At **St Nicholas's church**, in the village centre, there stands a solitary military headstone remembering Corporal Mollie Williams of the Women's Auxiliary Air Force, who died on 5 June 1944; when the RAF pulled out in 1958, an oak wall cabinet was presented to the church in memory of the association between the military and civilian communities, and this is now positioned in the church vestry.

Finally, on the wall in the entrance corridor at the **Square & Compass public house** can be seen an old 'RAF Worth Matravers' road direction sign and, on the wall in the snug bar, an abbreviated history of the airfield.

INDUSTRY

CHRISTCHURCH EXPERIMENTAL BRIDGING ESTABLISHMENT

OS: SZ 148931

Location: Barrack Road, Christchurch.

When members of the Royal Engineers were posted to Christchurch Barracks late in 1918 to form an Experimental Bridging Company (to produce equipment strong enough to carry the Army's recently introduced tanks), they set in motion work at Christchurch that has continued to this day on similar bridging matters and a whole host of other loosely associated activities. The barracks at which they were based was built at the end of the 18th century to house cavalry and horse-drawn artillery units, but was acquired by the Ministry of Supply in 1939 and not used as Army accommodation during the Second World War.

Having been run down to virtually skeleton manning during the inter-war years, a major expansion programme was started in 1938 as war clouds gathered over Europe and for the next seven or so years Christchurch was heavily involved in producing bridging equipment for the Allied forces. The resident design engineer, D. C. Bailey (later Sir Donald Bailey), drew up plans for the famous

The site today, parts of which would still be recognisable to those who worked here 50 or more years ago.

Bailey Bridge - which immediately made all other similar bridges in use obsolete - and before the war drew to a close over 600 firms in the British Isles were involved in Bailey Bridge construction, with over 200 miles of fixed and 40 miles of floating bridges being produced - some of which are still in use worldwide today. The 'Scissors' bridge carried on Churchill tanks was a Christchurch invention, while other projects touched on tugs, assault craft, earth-moving and road-making plant, fuel pipelines and the like.

Post-war the facility has been involved in, amongst other things, designing 'field runway' surfaces (including pads for use by VTOL Harrier aircraft), water purification apparatus and, of course, improvements to existing military bridges - the most successful of which was the 1960s Medium Girder Bridge, now marketed by Fairey Engineering Ltd and in use in over 50 countries in both military and civil guises.

As part of the Government's reduction in this country's fighting strength and research and development capabilities, the main part of the site was taken out of commission in 1994 and the remaining personnel - now part of the Defence Research Agency (DRA) - moved into a small enclave on the south of the site next to the River Stour, where a small dock facility has been retained.

Today plans have been laid for civil development of the abandoned area, but until this takes place the wartime buildings (and the old barracks) can still be seen from Barrack Road. The viewpoint of ongoing DRA activities that is easiest of access is the road bridge over the railway line near Christchurch station; however, even better views can be obtained from trains running past the site or from the River Stour itself.

The DRA dock on the banks of the River Stour.

POOLE BOAT YARDS OS: SZ 015903 (J. Bolson); SY 987904 (Dorset Yacht Co)

> Location: Bolson's shipyard is located in New Quay Road; that of the Dorset Yacht Co is in Lake Drive, both in Hamworthy.

During the Second World War the boat yards on the shores of Poole Harbour were to play a vital part in the war effort in turning out their share of the craft that were needed to stave off defeat, then to advance to final victory. The Hamworthy firm of J. Bolson & Son Ltd was already a well-established local company, specialising in pleasure craft building and in operating cruises for holidaymakers, when war broke out. Thus it was an ideal source of requisitioned craft for the new RN personnel at Poole, and for the manufacture of smaller vessels for military use.

Bolson's built a series of harbour defence launches, motor minesweepers and motor fishing vessels (MFVs) for the Navy, and was then directed to the manufacture of LCAs (landing craft, assault) in preparation for offensive operations. An acute shortage of LCAs and similar vessels was one of the fears that plagued both Churchill and Mountbatten, and only supreme efforts by firms such as Bolson were able to lay these very real fears to rest, with about 150 such craft being launched from Bolson's Poole yards prior to D-Day.

In friendly rivalry with Bolson & Son was the Dorset Yacht Company, based at Lake Drive in Hamworthy, who had built a series of motor torpedo boats, launches and MFVs for the Navy before also being directed towards LCA construction. Other local firms, not necessarily with any maritime experience, were engaged in the building of Mulberry Harbour sections, including the workforces of Newman's, Sydenham's and Burt & Vick's.

In addition to construction work, the local yards, working around the clock, carried out battle damage and other repairs, together with a whole series of modification programmes to enhance ships' fighting abilities.

Both the Dorset Yacht Co and Bolson & Son quickly slipped back into peacetime routine, Bolson's converting three landing craft to pleasure cruisers for their own use until dedicated craft for the task could be acquired, and today the shipyards are still active. The Dorset Yacht Company's yard no longer boasts the six slipways that it possessed in the 1940s and is now mainly involved with pleasure craft, while Bolson's continues to associate itself more with commercial and other small craft. Good views of Sydenham's complex can be obtained from the footpaths on Poole Bridge.

Bolson's Shipyard today, with Royal Marine landing craft being overhauled.

ROYAL NAVY CORDITE FACTORY

OS: SY 943904 (current site entrance)

Location: Alongside the A351 road,
between Wareham and Poole.

Built during the first two years of the Great War and opened in January 1916, the site for the RNCF was chosen on Holton Heath because of it being an area of flat land, with one small hill in the middle for a reservoir, and a large enough local population to provide a workforce. It was also clear of major built-up areas and next to a main railway line - the LSWR line from Waterloo to Weymouth. Its main tasks were the production of flashless cordite and Tetryl HE for naval guns. In 1931 a tragic explosion occurred at the establishment on the site known as Nitro Glycerine Hill, with ten workers being killed.

The factory boasted an extensive narrow gauge (2 ft 6 in) and standard gauge (4 ft 8½ in) railway system, a pier at the entrance to Lytchett Bay for the shipment in and out of materials, and a full range of support facilities, such as a massive generating plant, with 24 Lancashire boilers for steam production and four steam turbines for reserve electricity supply, and a well-equipped hospital.

In 1938 the site was extended as part of the nation's Rearmament Programme and was in full production again when hostilities commenced a year later. The RNCF was considered as a major strategic site and was thus very heavily defended - both by HAA and LAA batteries and the provision of Decoy Sites on Arne Heath and at Decoy Heath (named after a duck decoy once sited there!) - respectively south-east and west of the establishment. The former particularly proved its worth on the night of 3 June 1942, when over 200 bombs were dropped on it. On the late evening of 24 April 1940, however, the plant received hits from incendiary bombs, but the internal fire brigade quickly extinguished the flames. The RNCF provided its own Home Guard unit, both for site defence and the manning of the decoys.

A general view of the Administrative Block and former main entrance gate. The ship's figurehead is from the frigate HMS *Rattlesnake* (1822-1860).

With the war in Europe and the Far East won, the RNCF was placed on a care and maintenance status in April 1946, but reopened in November of the same year to meet a need for the production of the cordite component picric. Although a new lease of life was granted in 1952, when the production of rocket propellant for the Seaslug missile was started, the plant began its final rundown in 1957 and today only a relatively small area still has military connections - a unit of the Defence Research Agency being located there. The majority of the old site has been turned into a nature reserve (opened in 1981), while land near to the railway line is being utilised as an industrial estate - with some of the old buildings having been granted a stay of execution from the bulldozer and sledgehammer. The railway station originally built to serve the factory is still in use (but is closed on Sundays).

The best way to view the site today is to take the minor road off the A351 opposite the Texaco garage - signposted 'Defence Research Agency' - and observe, behind the distinctive black iron railings that still abound, the former Administrative Block (note the ship's figurehead) and other buildings on your left *en route* to the current main entrance, opposite which - on the other side of the road - note the refuge for air raids or internal threats still standing (near the bicycle racks). The building directly facing today's guardroom was once the site hospital.

The next buildings passed on your left include changing rooms, workshops and the former steam loco shed; on the Holton Heath Industrial Park note the massive old Generating Station and Boiler House, together with the former buildings of the guncotton factory. Finally, as you travel back towards the main road along Blackhill Road, note on your left glimpses of the old buildings in the trees where the picric factory was located.

(See also entries on Holton Heath LAA Gun Towers, page 47, and Holton Heath pillbox, page 64.)

The former Generating Station (left) and Boiler House, now on the Holton Heath Estate.

ROYAL ORDNANCE FACTORY, CREEKMOOR

OS: SZ 002942

Location: Sopers Lane, which lies to the west of the A349 Poole to Wimborne Minster Road, half a mile north of the Fleetsbridge Roundabout, Poole.

Major expansion of the national Royal Ordnance Factory organisation began in 1935, and work started on the building of an ordnance factory on a 35-acre site on the outskirts of Poole in 1939, the facility becoming operational in the following year (one of ten similar sites so to do). An idea of the importance of the ROF and Ministry of Supply armament-associated organisation to the war effort can be gauged by the fact that 206 new factories were built between April 1936 and September 1945 at a cost of over £285 million!

The Creekmoor site was protected by three pillboxes and a unit of the local Home Guard, and large enough to warrant its own railway system, known locally as the Creekmoor Light Railway, which joined the main Southern Railway's track on the Poole side of Creekmoor Halt (Broadstone Way now follows the line of the old trackbed).

The factory was involved primarily in the manufacturing of light weapons, with the bulk of its output being Oerlikon and Polsten 20 mm cannon - the latter being a

The factory today, as seen from Sopers Lane. All the buildings seen in this view are of Second World War vintage.

simplified and cheaper version of its better-known Swiss contemporary, and which went into production in 1942. So great was the demand for its products that the factory was working a continuous 24-hour shift system from 1941.

One unusual structure on the site was know colloquially as 'the tunnel', a long, hardened building in which the guns made here were tested for accuracy and alignment before being dispatched to military units. This was really the equivalent of the gun harmonising butts to be found on operational airfields.

Before the final cessation of hostilities, the manufacturing facilities were directed away from war work, and ceramic components initially for the cotton industry and later domestic housing were produced at Creekmoor. In the post-war years there have been a variety of users of the site, with the electronics companies Siemens plc and GPT Ltd being the present residents, and both producing a wide range of advanced products for civilian and defence use. Products currently leaving the works in Sopers Lane include such items as railway communications apparatus, traffic lights and control units, telephone exchange systems and a wide range of advanced electronic equipment for the armed forces.

It is not possible to gain access to the site today; nevertheless, from the roads outside one can see - on the 27 acres of the original site still retained by Siemens plc - that a very large number of the wartime buildings have been adopted and converted for ongoing use - sensitively restored, rather than flattened by the bulldozer! The three pillboxes remain standing and two very short sections of standard gauge railway line are still to be found in the middle of the site. With 1,200 employees, the electronics industry at Creekmoor is as important to the local Dorset economy today as the Ordnance Factory was to the war effort over 50 years ago.

One of the wartime pillboxes still in situ, together with a lifting gantry of the same vintage.

WHITEHEADS TORPEDO FACTORY AND BINCLEAVES TEST FACILITIES

OS: SY 667763 (Whiteheads);
SY 683783 (Bincleaves)

> Location: The former torpedo factory buildings are at Ferrybridge, Wyke Road, Weymouth (at the northern end of the isthmus joining Weymouth to Portland); the Bincleaves Test Facilities are on the northern and central arms of the Portland Breakwaters.

A torpedo factory was opened on an 8-acre site at Wyke Regis, Weymouth, in 1891, with a 1,000-yard pier, served by a compressed air railway system, constructed out into the waters of what would later become Portland Harbour. Vickers and Armstrong Whitworth were the majority shareholders in the business, but control was devolved to the Admiralty during the Great War, then reverted to Vickers Armstrong at the war's end. With no new orders on the books, the company went in to liquidation in 1921; however, the factory reopened as the Whitehead Torpedo Co Ltd in 1923, involved in the development of a range of torpedoes and mines.

A major modernisation took place in

A general view of the works today, with the trackbed of the former railway line to Portland running behind the factory.

1934. A firing point was built on the northern arm of the harbour breakwaters at Bincleaves, and from then onwards firings were conducted both into Weymouth Bay (the 'Distant Range') and, for acceptances and the like, across Portland Harbour. It was also in 1934 that the Royal Navy placed its first new orders for torpedoes.

On the outbreak of the Second World War the Admiralty requisitioned all foreign orders at Ferrybridge and placed its own new contracts. At the height of the invasion scare some of the workforce was dispersed to sites at Bournemouth, Street and Staines, and the factory and firing range were guarded by Whitehead's own Home Guard Unit. The factory was a target for the Luftwaffe on more than one occasion, the greatest damage being caused during a raid on 1 May 1941.

Throughout the war years Whitehead's made a major contribution to the national effort. In 1944, for example, the factory was producing three versions of the 18-inch torpedo and five of the 21-inch, together with a range of sea mines. One point of interest is that in 1944 timbers were stored to the rear of the factory to be used to turn the railway line to Portland across Small Mouth (OS: SY 668762) into a roadway should the only other road to the 'Overlord' embarkation port have been closed by enemy or any other action.

At the war's end the Admiralty invoked its contractual break clause, the last torpedoes and mines on order being delivered in 1946. In the post-war years work continued on torpedo research and production and other military projects, but gradually the emphasis changed from weapons of war to tools of peace. The last torpedo firing from Bincleaves took place in 1966.

A number of engineering companies have used the Ferrybridge factory since Vickers moved its Hydraulics Division here in 1959, but the last left in 1993; the site awaits redevelopment, and I do sincerely hope that when the historic factory buildings are finally razed to the ground that there will still be some reminder here of the site's important role in the two sad wars of the 20th century.

The best views of the buildings are obtained from the old staff car park, behind Ferrybridge Cottages, and from the footpath almost opposite the Ferrybridge Inn. Meanwhile at Bincleaves military R&D work continues, the facilities now being occupied by the Defence Research Agency. Good views of these buildings can be obtained from Weymouth's Nothe Gardens and the footpath leading from there towards ancient Sandsfoot Castle, and, of course, from the waters both inside and outside Portland Harbour.

The 'Distant Range' building, with defensive structure on the breakwater in the foreground and Weymouth Harbour Pier and seafront buildings beyond.

MEMORIALS

ADRIAN VAN DE WEYER MEMORIAL STONE

OS: SY 775932

> Location: On the edge of woodland
> 1 mile north of Tincleton.

2nd Lieutenant Adrian Van de Weyer, of the Rifle Brigade, was the youngest child of the Van de Weyer family, owners of Clyffe House, near Tincleton, and was killed during the gallant defence of Calais - which was pivotal to the success of the evacuation of the British Expeditionary Force from the beaches of Dunkirk. As a lad, Adrian loved to wander around the family estate, and particularly cherished the view south and westwards from the hilltop where his memorial stone now stands.

The stone, which bears the inscription

'Adrian Van de Weyer, Rifle Brigade, Calais, May 26th 1940', is best reached by following the public footpath that climbs up the hillside past Admiston Farm off the road running southwards from Puddletown to Tincleton.

2nd Lieutenant Van de Weyer now lies, with 224 of his fallen British and Commonwealth comrades, in the civil Calais Southern Cemetery, on the outskirts of the French town that he so bravely fought for.

At Tincleton church (OS: SY 776918) he is remembered on the village's Roll of Honour and on a plaque in his memory on the church wall.

The Van de Weyer stone. He, too, loved to walk up to this site with the family dogs.

COMMONWEALTH WAR GRAVES COMMISSION CEMETERIES

In 210 cemeteries and churchyards, and one crematorium, within the county of Dorset there lay buried or commemorated 705 casualties of the Second World War: 178 Navy personnel, 294 Army personnel, 195 Air Force personnel, 24 members of the merchant marine, and 14 members of the Home Guard and civilians. Of this total, 23 are unidentified. In addition to the War Graves Commission plots, one will occasionally find the final resting place of military personnel in individual or family graves in other Dorset cemeteries.

The vast majority of German personnel who were initially buried in Dorset were later re-interred in the German Cemetery at Cannock Chase in Staffordshire; the Brookwood Military Cemetery in Surrey was the final resting place for most Italian personnel who died in this country.

PORTLAND ROYAL NAVY CEMETERY
OS: SY 692740

> Location: Well-signposted, the cemetery lies at the end of a public footpath off Verne Common Road.

Beautifully maintained, and situated on a level strip of land below the massive northern face of the Isle of Portland with views out over the dockyard and Portland Harbour, this peaceful cemetery brings to mind the many Royal Commonwealth War Graves Commission Cemeteries that are 'forever a corner of Britain' all over the world. The Cross of Remembrance dates back to the years after the First World War.

There are 103 Second World War graves in the cemetery: 75 sailors, 11 soldiers, one coastguard, one merchant sea-

The grave of Jack Mantle VC, winner of the first Royal Navy Victoria Cross to be awarded for bravery within British territorial waters. Behind stands the Cemetery's Cross of Remembrance.

Two of the German airmen buried at Portland.

man, one sailor from the Royal Canadian Navy and another from the Royal New Zealand Navy, and one merchant seaman from Norway. Twelve German airmen are also laid to rest here.

While in no way drawing praise and appreciation away from all who lie here who gave their lives for our freedom today, of special interest is the grave of Leading Seaman Jack Mantle, who was posthumously awarded the Victoria Cross for his bravery when he continued to man his gun on the auxiliary AA ship HMS *Foylebank* as she was overwhelmed by German JU 87s on 7 July 1940. Jack Mantle was a Dorset lad, spending his

childhood years at Affpuddle, but as his family moved to Southampton in later years, his name does not appear on the Affpuddle village war memorial.

A recent addition to the cemetery is the memorial stone moved here in May 1995 from the naval base, in anticipation of its closure, in memory of HMS *Osprey* personnel who have lost their lives in more modern times. It was originally commissioned following the loss of the Ship's Flight helicopter of HMS *Brilliant* off Vipingo, Kenya, on 14 May 1989, and contains seven names - six members of the Royal Navy and one member of the Royal Fleet Auxiliary.

SHAFTESBURY CEMETERY

OS: ST 872228

Location: Mampitts Road, a turning off Linden Park, the first road off the A350 north of the Royal Chase roundabout on the Shaftesbury ring road.

The military plot in the town's civilian cemetery lies in its south-west corner, approached through a lych gate that was a gift to the town from 'the Shaftesbury and District Royal British Legion Women's Branch in proud memory of those who

gave their lives in the service of their country, 1939-1945'.

The Allied graves are of 26 British soldiers and one airman, together with one Polish soldier and, even further away from his homeland, a private from the Soviet forces. Additionally, there are three German combatants buried here (one soldier, one sailor and one airman) and six Italian soldiers. On reading the headstones, one's attention is drawn to the fact that a small number of the dates of passing away are just post-war - an indication of the prisoner-of-war camps and military hospitals located nearby. **Motcombe Park** (OS: ST 850240) is an example of the former, and the **United States Army Hospital at Guy's Marsh** (OS: ST 845206) an example of the latter.

There is one further Second World War military grave, remote from the others, towards the north-east corner of the cemetery, quite near to the lych gate.

The beautifully tended military plot at Shaftesbury, and Soviet Private Duschin's headstone.

SHERBORNE CEMETERY

OS: ST 631160

Location: Lenthay Road, on the western outskirts of Sherborne.

There are 31 burial plots from the Second World War in the War Graves Commission area at this civilian cemetery, laid out in two groups - one naval and the other Army and RAF - close to the main entrance gate, consisting of 12 sailors, nine soldiers and five airmen from the armed forces of the United Kingdom, together with one Home Guard volunteer, two members of the Royal New Zealand

In the rear row of the Army and RAF plot stands the headstone at the grave of Home Guard Volunteer H. E. Sweet. Most unusually for a known person, neither his age nor his date of birth are recorded.

Navy, one member of the Royal Netherlands Navy and a single civilian (an ex-serviceman, but not a Second World War casualty). Additionally, there are 25 Great War burials and a number of graves from the post-war period.

The cemetery itself was also a war 'casualty', for the superintendent's house and the previous main gates were destroyed during an air raid on 30 September 1940. The graves were undamaged.

In the school sports field on the opposite side of the road from the main gate, note the above-ground air raid shelter - later utilised as a changing room, but now little used.

WARMWELL (HOLY TRINITY) CHURCHYARD

OS: SY 753858

Location: On the B3390 from Warmwell Cross to Crossways.

This churchyard contains 23 burials from the 1939-45 war: one soldier and 20 airmen from the UK, one airman from the RCAF and a Polish airman. Two of the RAF personnel remain unidentified. Of the airmen buried here, 11 are pilots, six of whom fell during the Battle of Britain; the most senior is Squadron Leader T. G. Lovell-Gregg of 87 Sqn, RAF Exeter, who crashed near Abbotsbury on 15 August 1940 (at the height of the Battle of Britain) while trying to reach Warmwell aerodrome after being shot down in combat over Portland Harbour. The youngest burial is of Private W. A. Hayes of the Dorsetshire Regiment, who died on 11 November 1941, aged just 17 years, when a Hurricane aircraft crashed on the ammunition dump that he was guarding. One of the graves is of a member of the Women's Auxiliary Air Force, LACW Eileen Riley.

Above **A general view of the War Graves Commission plot, with the headstone of Czechoslovak pilot Sergeant Jaroslav Hlavac RAFVR, shot down over Wareham, in the foreground.**

Right **The grave of Squadron Leader Terence Lovell-Gregg, behind which can be seen (left to right) the graves of Pilot Officer Lancelot Sandes DFC, Private William Hayes and that of one of the two unidentified RAF men who are buried here.**

CRANBORNE PARISH CHURCH: COLOURS OF THE 2nd SEARCHLIGHT BATTALION

OS: SU 054133

Location: The Church of
St Mary & St Bartholomew, Cranborne.

The Regimental Standard of the 2nd Searchlight Regiment, Royal Artillery - together with the Union Flag - proudly adorn the South wall of this parish church. Alongside there is a plaque commemorating the association between the officers and men of the Regiment and the church and village, together with the ecclesiastical insignia worn by the Reverend L. F. Addison during his time as the Regiment's Chaplain. An annual reunion service is still held in the church, and in addition to the plaque and a lectern given to the church on the Regiment's disbandment, gifts for the church were given again in 1970 and 1977.

The Regimental Colours.

The commemorative plaque and certificate, together with the Padre's insignia.

DICK BEARD MEMORIAL, COMPTON ACRES GARDENS

OS: SZ 053896

Location: Compton Acres Gardens, situated in Canford Cliffs Road, Canford Cliffs; well signposted.

Shortly after the Great War Mr Thomas Simpson bought 12½ acres of rough land overlooking Poole Harbour and the Purbecks and set out to build an extensive dream garden, laid out in such a way that no one individual garden would be overlooked from another, and each of which would be styled completely differently from its neighbours. The gardens enjoyed royal patronage and were immensely popular. Sadly, the calls upon manpower of the Second World War resulted in the high standards that the gardens enjoyed falling away and, by the time hostilities ceased, the site was almost completely overgrown.

Luckily, a saviour was found in London architect Mr J. S. Beard, who bought the gardens in 1950 and reopened them in May 1952, since when they have gone from strength to strength. Many now consider them to be the finest formal gardens in all of Europe.

It is Beard's only son, Dick, who provides us with the link between Compton Acres Gardens and the Second World War, for Flight Lieutenant Richard Beard was killed while flying on active service with the Royal Air Force in 1942. In 1957 a Garden of Memory was dedicated here to Dick, and to his two sisters, both of whom died of polio. His name lives on in this beautiful spot in the form of a teak garden seat - the centre one of the three - bearing the simple inscription 'Dick Beard 1922-1944'.

The gardens are open to the public from 1 March to 31 October, from 10.30 am to 6.30 pm (or dusk, if earlier).

The Garden of Memory. Moving, and most appropriate, words are engraved on the stone at the rear the arbour: 'To live on in the hearts of those we love is not to die'.

DORCHESTER TOWN WAR MEMORIAL

OS: SY 693904

> Location: At the junction of
> South Walks Road and Trinity Street.

The War Memorial for the county town of Dorchester, based upon the design of the Cenotaph in Whitehall and similarly built of Portland stone, stands at the junction of the town's main shopping street and, in contrast, the peaceful tree-lined South Walks Road.

Originally designed to honour the town's fallen in 'the war to end all wars',

it was dedicated on Empire Day 1921 and bore 237 names. Additional tablets, however, were added in 1948 and 1949 and bear the names of 81 Dorchester combatants who gave their lives in the Second World War. Peace in the world still eludes us, and further names have had to be added commemorating those who have died in post-1945 conflicts.

The Dorchester War Memorial - on this occasion proudly bearing wreaths laid on Remembrance Sunday.

DURWESTON FOREST MEMORIAL STONE TO PILOT OFFICER JOHN ALLEN

OS: SY 833064

Location: In Field Grove, part of the Durweston Forest 3½ miles west of Blandford Forum.

Pilot Officer John Allen, a 19-year-old Spitfire pilot with No 152 Squadron, crashed on 29 November 1940 after being scrambled to intercept a German fighter sweep; his aircraft fell at this spot and it is thought that his sad death followed a failure of his oxygen equipment rather than as a direct result of enemy action.

Over the years two plaques were attached to a tree near where he fell, then in 1977 the local branch of the Royal Air Forces Association placed a granite memorial stone here in his memory. A service of remembrance is held annually in the glade, known locally as Field Grove, where he died. A smaller plaque commemorates his father, who also served in the Royal Air Force.

To locate the stone, walk eastward up the bridleway (signposted 'Bryanston') from Hedge End Farm, located on the minor road from Winterborne Whitechurch to Okeford Fitzpaine, until you pass below a line of power cables. Almost immediately enter the trees on your left by a narrow (but well-defined) pathway, and keep to your left on reaching a wider path. Continue along here, following the forest edge on your left, until you reach an area where the foliage is obviously not natural, consisting of planted shrubs and fir trees. The stone will be on your right-hand side, just off the trail. This is about a 10-minute walk from the power lines.

The Pilot Officer Allen Memorial Stone.

PILOT HIGHT ROAD, KINSON

OS: SZ 062957

Location: To the east of Poole Lane, Kinson. (From Poole Lane proceed along Turbary Park and Mandale Roads until reaching Pilot Hight Road.)

The road name in Pilot Hight Road.

At 6.15 pm on 15 August 1940 Spitfire R6988 of No 234 Sqn based at RAF Middle Wallop was shot down by enemy fighters escorting a formation of bomber aircraft and crashed in Bournemouth. The pilot, 22-year-old New Zealander Pilot Officer Cecil Henry Hight, baled out of his stricken aircraft but, sadly, his parachute did not open; it may have been, of course, that he was too badly wounded to pull the D-ring.

Pilot Hight Road is named after this young man; a man who came from far away in the Commonwealth and gave his life for freedom. He is buried in Bournemouth East Cemetery, in 1940 located in Hampshire.

PORTLAND AND WEYMOUTH D-DAY PORT MEMORIALS

PORTLAND

OS: SY 684737

> Location: Victoria Gardens, Fortuneswell.

This handsome block of Portland stone, with a brass plaque affixed, commemorates the vital part played in the success of the D-Day landings and subsequent follow-up operations by the port facilities provided at Portland. The main text reads:

'The major part of the American assault force which landed on the shores of France on "D" Day, 6 June 1944, was launched from Portland Harbor. From 6 June 1944 to 7 May 1945, 418,585 troops and 144,093 vehicles were embarked from this harbor. This plaque marks the route which the vehicles and troops took on their way to the points of embarkation.'

The memorial was unveiled by the American Ambassador, John G. Winant, during a ceremony on the afternoon of 22 August 1945; at the same time the former Cadets Road was renamed Victory Road.

The memorial in Victoria Gardens, Portland.

WEYMOUTH

> Location: Weymouth Esplanade, opposite the Royal Hotel.

Highlighting both the part played by Weymouth as a port of embarkation and the transit facilities provided by the town, the memorial in Weymouth is of a completely different design from that in Portland; it is a different shape entirely and has a light on the top that is permanently illuminated. The text, on a brass tablet, is similar to that at Portland, the exact wording being:

'The major part of the American Assault Force which landed on the shores of France 6 June 1944 was launched from Weymouth & Portland Harbors. From 6 June 1944 to 7 May 1945, 517,816 troops & 144,093 vehicles embarked from the harbors. Many of the troops left from Weymouth Pier. The remainder of the troops and all vehicles passed through Weymouth en route to Portland points of embarkation.'

Both monuments pay fitting tribute to the important part played by these two towns and their ports in the liberation of Europe. Sadly, many of those who set off

A night-time view of Weymouth's Memorial, the light on which is never switched off. On the opposite side of the road is the Royal Hotel, which served as the port's D-Day Embarkation HQ.

from here were destined to die on the eastern of the two American landing beaches - 'Bloody Omaha'.

RHODES-MOORHOUSE MEMORIAL, PARNHAM

OS: ST 472005

Location: High ground to the rear
of Parnham House
(see separate entry, page 59).

Within the confines of the grave of the father he never knew - William Rhodes-Moorhouse VC RFC, the first airman to be awarded the Victoria Cross, who died of wounds on 27 April 1915 - lie the ashes of Flight Lieutenant William Henry Rhodes-Moorhouse DFC RAF.

In the face of overwhelming odds, the younger Rhodes-Moorhouse, flying Hurricanes with No 601 (County of London) Squadron, was shot from the Kentish skies above Royal Tunbridge Wells on the morning of 6 September 1940 and joined so many of his contemporaries as but a cherished memory of a gallant young man.

His father's dying wish had been to be buried at the family home; it was only right and proper, therefore, that his son, one of the Battle of Britain's brave 'Few', should return to Dorset and share his final resting place with him.

The small burial ground is on private farmland; nevertheless, it can be clearly seen from the public footpath that runs from the back of Parnham House, via a wooden bridge across the River Brit, towards the village of Stoke Abbott.

The Rhodes-Moorhouse Memorial.

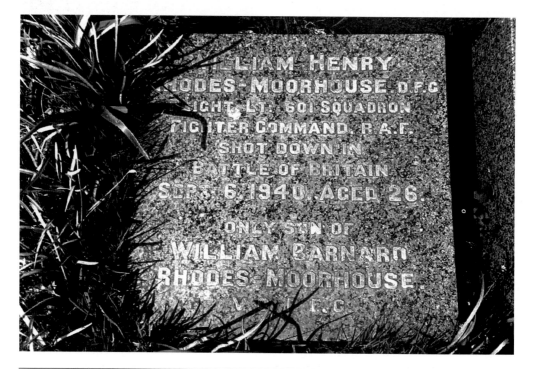

ROYAL ARMOURED CORPS MEMORIAL, BINDON HILL OS: SY 833803

Location: On Bindon Hill, within the Lulworth Ranges Danger Area, just to the east of Lulworth Cove and only accessible when the range walks are open to the public.

With dramatic views, both to seaward and northwards across the Frome Valley towards the Lulworth and Bovington Camps, this simple stone memorial stands at a place of outstanding natural beauty. The east face of the memorial bears the badge of the Royal Armoured Corps; the inscription on the west face bears a dedication to those who gave their lives while serving with the Corps.

(The defensive position shown on the rear cover is located just below this monument on the cliff edge.)

The Royal Armoured Corps Memorial Stone.

ST JAMES'S CHURCH, POOLE (US COAST GUARD MEMORIAL)

OS: SZ 008904

Location: St James's church, which is signposted as 'Parish Church' from the Old Town and Quay areas of Poole.

The beautiful Georgian church of St James - the Parish Church of Poole - contains a number of commemorative items associated with the Second World War. The memorial to the United States Coast Guard is in the form of a plaque to the rear of the pulpit, above which flies an American flag - the Stars and Stripes - from a rescue cutter based at Poole for the D-Day landings. As the plaque indicates, Rescue Flotilla One saved more than 1,400 Allied troops from the English Channel during landing operations.

Also hanging in the church, and of wartime vintage, are the flags of the Fire Service and the Royal British Legion, while on the south wall of the body of the church there is a brass plaque in memory of Flight Lieutenant Peter Joliffe RAF, who was killed in action over Norway on 24 June 1940.

Finally, in the entrance to the church and above the Parish's Great War Memorial, visitors to this haven of peace in the centre of bustling Poole should note the town's Second World War Roll of Honour. It commemorates 10 members of the Royal Navy, 20 of the Army, nine of the Royal Air Force and 11 members of the Merchant Navy who gave their lives in the quest for victory over the tyranny of Nazi Germany, Fascist Italy and Imperial Japan.

The church is open to the public whenever a guide is in attendance (which is for most of the time during the tourist season); at other times, sadly, it has to be kept locked.

The United States Coastguard Memorial Plaque.

ST JOHN'S CHURCH, PORTLAND (COLOURS OF THE 14th PORT REGIMENT, US ARMY)

OS: SY 686735

Location: St John's church, Fortuneswell, Portland.

As a memento of its close association with the people of Portland, both service and civilian, the 14th Major Port Regiment presented its Stars and Stripes colours to St John's church when it left the island on completion of its mammoth task supporting the D-Day landings and the subse-quent reinforcement of the European Theatre of Operations.

With a small plaque affixed below, the colours are proudly displayed on the church's wall - opposite the Roll of Honour, which is itself bedecked with a pair of white ensigns.

With the Royal Naval Association colours next to it, the commemorative Stars and Stripes fly proudly from the church wall.

ST MICHAEL'S CHURCH, HAMWORTHY (ROYAL MARINES MEMORIAL)

OS: SY 994912

Location: St Michael's church, Blandford Road, Hamworthy.

The lych gate at Hamworthy's St Michael's church was erected by Royal Marine veterans in memory of their fallen comrades and contains two commemorative plaques. One reads:

'This lych gate was erected by surviving members of the Support Squadron, Eastern Flank, in honoured memory of all their Shipmates who lost their lives in the Assault on Walcheren Island on 1st November 1944.'

The attack on Walcheren was part of the efforts made to re-open Antwerp to the sea and allow troops and material supporting the assault on Germany to go directly into battle rather than have to face the long journey from Normandy. In addition to the Royal Marines, troops from the 1st Dorsets were also involved in the assault landings.

The other plaque carries the wording:

'Also in memory of earlier Squadron losses off the Normandy Beaches from 6th June to 28th August 1944.'

The lych gate at St Michael's, Hamworthy.

ST NICHOLAS'S CHURCH, ABBOTSBURY

OS: SY 578852

Location: The village of Abbotsbury, on the B3157 Weymouth to Bridport road.

The carnage was such in the Great War that the villages that were spared the death in service of even one of its inhabitants were very few and far between. So unusual was it, in fact, that these villages are still known today as the 'Thankful Villages'. This was not quite the case in the Second World War, so the plaque on the wall in the beautiful church of St Nicholas in rural Abbotsbury is quite unusual.

It hangs on the north wall of the nave, next to the Roll of Honour listing the 13 parishioners who gave their lives for their King and Country in the 1914-1918 conflict, and - as can be seen in the photograph - carries the following grateful text:

'We record with hearty thanks to Almighty God that during the course of The Second World War 1939-1945 no parishioners of Abbotsbury whether serving in His Majesty's Forces or remaining at home lost their lives by enemy action. 'Give thanks unto the Lord, for He is gracious and His mercy endureth for ever.'

This was, of course, true. Abbotsbury did, however, see a service death within its boundaries, for it was at Abbotsbury Swannery - between the village and Chesil Bank - that Squadron Leader 'Shovel' Gregg-Lovell was killed while attempting to carry out a forced landing in his battle-damaged Spitfire at the height of the Battle of Britain, on 15 August 1940. He lies buried at Warmwell Cemetery.

The plaque in Abbotsbury church.

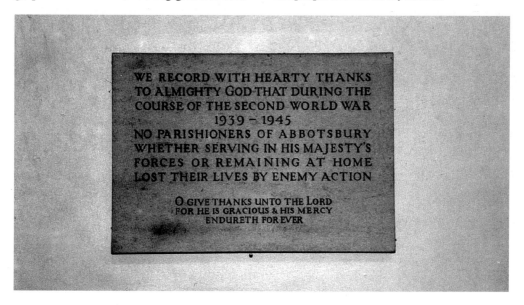

WE RECORD WITH HEARTY THANKS
TO ALMIGHTY GOD THAT DURING THE
COURSE OF THE SECOND WORLD WAR
1939 – 1945
NO PARISHIONERS OF ABBOTSBURY
WHETHER SERVING IN HIS MAJESTY'S
FORCES OR REMAINING AT HOME
LOST THEIR LIVES BY ENEMY ACTION

O GIVE THANKS UNTO THE LORD
FOR HE IS GRACIOUS & HIS MERCY
ENDURETH FOR EVER

SERGEANT ESSEX MEMORIAL SEAT, HURST HEATH

OS: SY 783896

Location: Hurst Heath, near Moreton.

Sergeant Ronald William Essex, aged 30 years at the time of his death, was a true son of Dorset, leaving behind him in Dorchester both his parents and his wife Mary. He was killed in the Battle of El Alamein, one of the most decisive battles of the Second World War, and has no known final resting place, his name being amongst the 11,874 that are listed on the Alamein Memorial as having no known grave (of whom 8,392 died in the Western Desert).

The seat erected here in his memory bears the inscription:

'In loving memory of Sergt R W Essex, 50th Tank Regiment. Killed at El Alemain (sic) Nov 2nd 1942, aged 30 years. He loved and spent many happy hours here.'

The seat is located on an S-bend on the minor road between Moreton and Woodsford, less than a quarter of a mile west of its crossroads junction with the B3390, and is approached through a conspicuous pair of wooden gateposts

The Sergeant Essex Memorial Seat.

SHERBORNE ABBEY

OS: ST 638165

Location: In the centre of the town of Sherborne.

In and around historic Sherborne Abbey stand memorials to the Dorsetshire Regiment, members of the United States Army and local civilians.

The Abbey's Lady Chapel is also the Regimental Chapel of the old Dorsetshire (later Dorset) Regiment, and within it, and on the walls of the Abbey, are laid up all the traced Colours of the Regiment, below the stands of which are painted replicas of the Colours above and a brief regimental history for the period of that Colour.

The screen on the south wall of the Chapel commemorates the Dorsets' actions in the Second World War, complementing those dedicated to Great War losses. Six oak pews and two reading desks have also been presented to the Abbey by the personnel and veterans of the Regiment. In the Ambulatory beside the Chapel are three Rolls of Honour, one for each of the wars with Germany and the third of local casualties of war. The last of the Colours was laid up on 1 April 1967 by the late Duchess of Kent, then the Regiment's Colonel in Chief.

To the south of the Abbey, in Half Moon Street, stands the town's War Memorial, initially commissioned to pay tribute to Sherborne's Great War casualties. Attached to the wall to the rear of the memorial are five brass plaques remembering those who died in the Second

World War: two remember the town's servicemen (12 RN, 33 Army, nine RAF, one Home Guard and one merchant navy). The others are a little 'out of the ordinary':

Civilian Air Raid Casualties Sherborne suffered Dorset's worst inland air raid of the war, when on 30 September 1940 some 60 bombs were dropped on the town and 18 people were killed. The Luftwaffe's target had been the Westland aircraft factory at Yeovil.

294th Engineer Battalion, US Army In the build-up to D-Day, American forces were based within the grounds of Sherborne Castle (in addition to those at

The Ambulatory at the entrance to the Dorsets' Regimental Chapel.

the military hospital in Haydon Park, south of the Castle). Around lunchtime on 30 March 1944 a massive explosion occurred when a lorry ran over an anti-tank mine during a training exercise, and 29 members of C Company of the 294th Engineer Battalion were killed. One of the two United States plaques commemorates these casualties, and the one next to it is dedicated to the memory of other members of the Battalion who died in the subsequent fighting from Normandy to central Germany. Both were erected by their surviving comrades on 6 June 1989, the 45th Anniversary of the 'Overlord' landings.

The plaques around Sherborne's War Memorial, with the Abbey as backdrop. Of the upper plaques, the two on the left commemorate the town's Second World War military casualties and that on the right the civilian casualties of the September 1940 air raid. The lower two plaques are in memory of members of the US Army Engineers based locally.

TARRANT RUSHTON AIRFIELD MEMORIAL STONE

OS: ST 950062

> Location: Adjacent to the entrance to the old airfield, at a tight bend on the road along its northern boundary.

There are two memorial plaques mounted on a simple stone plinth by the entrance to the airfield. The top one commemorates all who operated from Tarrant Rushton airfield from 1943 to 1980, while the one below honours 'all who served with 298 & 644 Sqns, RAF, and C Sqn, Glider Pilot Regt'.

The second plaque pictures a Halifax aircraft towing a Hamilcar glider, probably the activity for which RAF Tarrant Rushton will be remembered more than anything else.

This well-tended site receives many visits by veterans of Tarrant Rushton's exciting years and is the annual scene of a memorial service.

The Tarrant Rushton Memorial Stone, with a wartime T2 hangar in the background.

RAF WARMWELL MEMORIAL STONE

OS: SY 767883

Location: Mount Skippet Way, Crossways (signposted off the B3390).

As the entry on RAF Warmwell reveals (page 113), this grass airfield made many important contributions to the nation's war effort, most especially during the Battle of Britain and during the campaign to wrest control of Europe back from the Nazis. Thus it is most appropriate that an impressive monument should now stand in memory of those who gave their lives while serving here.

The stone was unveiled on 11 June 1989 and is now in the care of Crossways Parish Council, which is very proud of its association with RAF Warmwell. The Council has erected an information board at the site, known as Memorial Park, and its Chairman's badge of office has a Spitfire aircraft as part of the design. The village hall (OS: SY 768880), which is kept locked when not in use, contains other memorabilia of RAF Warmwell.

The memorial stone and airfield information board, which are located approximately where the Operations Block once stood, with the Memorial Park in the background.

WIMBORNE MINSTER WAR MEMORIAL PLAQUE OS: SY 999999

> Location: Wimborne Abbey.

This plaque, bearing the names of 32 Wimborne Minster servicemen who fell during the 1939-45 war, is affixed to the wall of the South Transept of the Minster, with - in poignant recognition of their fallen comrades - the laid-up colours of the local branch of the Royal British Legion displayed on either side. The memorial is most unusual in that the dedication contains only Second World War names, and none from the Great War.

The Wimborne Minster War Memorial Plaque.

43rd (WESSEX) DIVISION MEMORIAL

OS: ST 491060

> Location: On high ground at Winyard's Gap on the A356 Dorchester to Crewkerne Road.

This memorial stone, a replica of the one on Point 112, the hill 5 miles south-west of Caen where the Division fought its first major battle in the Normandy Campaign, from 10 to 24 July 1944, is one of several unveiled in similar hilltop locations during 1952 (the nearest to this one being on Castle Hill, outside Mere in Somerset). It commemorates those of the Wessex Division who fell in the long and costly battles between the D-day landings and the arrival of the Division in the Baltic, in May 1945. The 43rd Wessex Division was involved in some of the heaviest fighting in the whole of the North West Europe Campaign, with its casualty list showing that 12,482 of its personnel were either killed, missing or wounded before VE Day.

Above the inscription - dedicated 'to the memory of all ranks of the 43rd Wessex Division who laid down their lives for freedom 1939 to 1945' - is a square plaque featuring the 43rd's Wyvern emblem, the most historically significant of all the Divisional emblem signs worn in the European Campaign, having first been carried into battle by King Alfred's troops in AD879.

To reach the memorial, turn off the A356 at the Winyards Gap Inn along the minor road leading to the village of Chedington. Access to the memorial is by steps and a path through attractive woodland from the small lay-by some 400 yards from the inn. The land is in the ownership of the National Trust; the views over Dorset and Somerset from the memorial are superb, often complemented by numbers of buzzards soaring overhead.

The 43rd (Wessex) Division Memorial.

MUSEUMS

MUSEUM OF COASTAL DEFENCE

Location: The Nothe Fort, Weymouth -
well signposted.
(Tel: 01305-787243/786025)

Open: Daily in summer months from
10.30 am to 5.30 pm; less often in spring,
autumn and winter.

The Museum of Coastal Defence is housed within the Nothe Fort complex (see separate entry, page 57) and contains over 30 large displays - many with sound and movement - with over 150 life-size figures, 11 dioramas and a multitude of ship, aircraft and armoured vehicle models, together with extensive photographic displays. All these combine to give the visitor a true appreciation of life and service in the fort over the years. Additionally, there is a range of guns on display on the ramparts and military vehicles on the main ground level area. The Second World War is particularly well represented.

Excellent views of Weymouth and Portland Harbours can be obtained from the ramparts; during summer Sunday afternoons band concerts are often given at the Nothe Fort. Admission prices are particularly reasonable and, all in all, the Museum of Coastal Defence is very well worth a visit.

Part of the RAF Room, which contains - with other excellent and comprehensive display material - the remains of one of the Bouncing Bomb prototypes, which were later used on the famous Dambusters Raid.

MILITARY MUSEUM OF DEVON AND DORSET

Location: Bridport Road, near the
Top o' Town roundabout, Dorchester.
(Tel: 01305-264066)

Open: Monday to Saturday
9.30 am to 5.00 pm.

Housed in the 19th-century Keep of the former Poundbury Barracks (see separate entry, page 72), the Regimental Museum of the Devonshire & Dorset Regiment - the senior English County Regiment - was reopened at Easter 1995 after an extensive facelift, and now provides an excellent panorama of 300 years of the military history of the Regiments before amalgamation, and as the single Regiment of modern times. It has excellent display areas, well supported by audio-visual presentations and inter-active information con-

soles, and contains many fascinating individual historic items.

The Second World War display is as extensive as any other in the Museum, with the desk 'rescued' by the Dorsets from the ruins of Hitler's Chancellery in the centre of ruined Berlin being of major historic value. The Second World War 25-pounder field gun on display on the ground floor is also of particular interest, as is the adjacent diorama featuring the Dorset's involvement in the Burma Campaign.

One additional bonus to be obtained from a visit to the Museum is the excellent view over the county town of Dorchester and the beautiful Dorset countryside from the castellated roof of the building. All of the military museums in the county are worth visiting; this one, though, has a true Dorset atmosphere to it.

Part of the Second World War display, with the desk from the Berlin Chancellery to the rear - together with 'liberated' German flags and portrait of Adolf Hitler.

ROYAL SIGNALS MUSEUM OF ARMY COMMUNICATIONS

Location: Blandford Army Camp - well
signposted. (Tel: 01258-482248)

Open: Monday to Friday (all year round)
10.00 am to 5.00 pm; weekends (June to
September) 10.00 am to 4.00 pm.

Located within the confines of Blandford Army Camp (see separate entry, page 34), this is a truly fine military museum, with its many interesting exhibits particularly clearly displayed and very well annotated. It contains items associated with Army communications from the Crimea War of 1854-1856 right up to the Gulf War of 1991 and the Army of today. The memorabilia of the Second World War is particularly fascinating, and includes a fine collection of spy radios. In the Second World War Gallery visitors can see a Willys Jeep adapted for use by troops of the 6th Airborne Division, and an armoured command vehicle in a real-

istic desert combat setting, while other Second World War artifacts are set in specialist display cabinets throughout the museum.

Of special Dorset interest is the particularly good dioramic model of the battle for the bridge over the Caen Canal (Pegasus Bridge), for the airborne troops involved departed for France from nearby RAF Tarrant Rushton. Additionally, there are a number of military motorcycles on display, as well as collections of uniforms, medals and light weapons, and a well-stocked shop.

In 1996 a major extension to the museum will open, which will include some of the larger vehicles that have served with the Royal Corps of Signals and its predecessors, together with a restaurant and other extensive display areas.

As with the other military museums within the county, the Museum of Army Communications is very well worth a visit, and I commend it to you.

Part of the interesting and informative Second World War Gallery.

TANK MUSEUM, BOVINGTON

> Location: Bovington Army Camp,
> near Wool - well signposted.
> (Tel: 01929-405096)
>
> Open: Daily 10.00 am to 5.00 pm.

The collection of armoured fighting vehicles and other associated vehicles and equipment at Bovington runs to over 260 exhibits and makes this one of the finest military museums and the largest tank museum open to the public in the world. The vehicle collection - spanning the period from the First World War up to the Gulf War and the armies of today - is complemented by detailed wall displays, videos and realistic scenic backdrops. Children (of all ages!) can climb on, and even enter, some of the exhibits. 'Special Events' are held throughout the year, the highlight of these being the Battle Day held in the summer. The museum has an excellent restaurant and gift shop.

Chieftain (left) and Churchill tanks stand guard at the museum entrance.

Armoured fighting vehicles of Second World War vintage on display in one of the cavernous exhibition halls.

PORTLAND MUSEUM

Location: 217, Wakeham, Portland.
(Telephone: 01305-821804)

Open: April to September 10.30 to 17.00
(closed 13.00 to 13.30);
October to March as above, but on
Fridays to Tuesdays only.

In addition to the county's four military museums, many of the other museums within Dorset have some exhibits associated with the Second World War. Perhaps the best of these is this small and attractive museum, of special interest to the military historian as it contains one particularly interesting Second World War artifact - one of the experimental 'Highball' bouncing bombs, which was dropped in The Fleet (the inland water between Chesil Beach and the mainland) during weapons trials. This was not one of the 'Upkeep' bombs used on the Dambusters Raid in May 1943, but an anti-shipping 'Highball' bomb of a type never used in anger. It was recovered from The Fleet on 30 September 1992, and a display on the bomb and its recovery is contained within the museum.

Other items of particular interest are based upon Portland's naval activity, in particular the sinking of HMS *Foylebank*, in which Jack Mantle (see page 129) won his Victoria Cross. The Museum's archives contain a collection of over 600 glass plate photographs from the Whiteheads Torpedo Works (see separate entry, page 125), and it has regular 'special displays', sometimes of a military theme, in its public rooms. All this, plus its display of shipwreck photographs (some of naval vessels), makes Portland Museum very well worth a visit.

A prototype bouncing bomb and display information board in the museum garden.